BUFFALO TIGER

Indians of the Southeast

BUFFALO TIGER

A Life in the Everglades

BUFFALO TIGER
and Harry A. Kersey Jr.

Buffalo Tiger

University of Nebraska Press

Lincoln and London

Library of Congress Cataloging-in-Publication Data

Buffalo Tiger, 1920–

Buffalo Tiger : a life in the Everglades / Buffalo Tiger and Harry A. Kersey Jr.

p. cm.— (Indians of the Southeast)

Includes bibliographical references and index.

ISBN 0-8032-1317-4 (cloth : alk. paper)

1. Buffalo Tiger, 1920– . 2. Mikasuki Indians—Biography. 3. Mikasuki Indians—Civil rights. 4. Mikasuki Indians—Government relations. I. Title: Life in the Everglades. II. Kersey, Harry A., 1935– III. Title. IV. Series.

E99.M615 B83 2002

975'. 004973—dc21   2001052235

To my wife, Yolima Tiger, with love and thanks for all the support you gave me, taking care of our small business and giving me time to work on this book. I respect you a great deal.   BUFFALO TIGER

To my wife, Ruth Dyer Kersey, who lovingly but firmly kept me focused on the work at hand.   HARRY A. KERSEY JR.

Contents

Illustrations

Series Editors' Introduction

Buffalo Tiger is a major contribution to the study of Native people in the Southeast. Buffalo Tiger spoke for the Miccosukees during the Seminoles' struggle against termination, he guided their separation from the Seminoles, he presided over their first constitutional government, and he helped develop the contracting system that became a model for the U.S. policy of Indian self-determination. His involvement in this tumultuous period in Native American history alone would make his autobiography valuable, but his story also includes the most detailed description of a Native belief system in the Southeast since James Mooney published the Cherokee stories and sacred formulas of Swimmer over a century ago. Tiger vividly describes life in the Everglades, an example of human adaptation and cultural persistence rarely matched. Tiger speaks for himself with historian Harry A. Kersey Jr. contributing only brief introductions to each chapter that help contextualize the narrative. In a substantial afterword following Tiger's autobiography, Kersey broadens the story into a compelling scholarly account of the Miccosukee struggle for political sovereignty and cultural integrity. In an appendix Kersey examines the genre of Native American autobiography and *Buffalo Tiger*'s place within it. This book is a welcome addition to the Indians of the Southeast series.

THEDA PERDUE

MICHAEL D. GREEN

Acknowledgments

I started this book project some time ago but was not able to locate the professional help needed to get it published. After many attempts I did manage to make arrangements with Dr. Harry A. Kersey Jr. He is a long-time friend of mine. He is an author and history professor. I met with Dr. Kersey while at a Florida Governor's Council meeting about having a book written and maybe we could get together. He said we could do it. We talked continuously. Then I went to Florida Atlantic University to see him—he's teaching there—to see when he could do the book. Then he said he was going on a trip to Africa. Then I heard he got sick, and I didn't talk to him for a long time. I ran into him again two years ago at the Miccosukee reservation during a special meeting. He had been hired as a consultant for the tribe. I told him, Let's go ahead and get the book going. We talked about three things: maybe a dictionary, a Florida Indian history book for schools, and a biography. He agreed with me to do a biography. He said he thought we should have gone with it a long time ago. I have confidence in him because I know he's knowledgeable about Miccosukee history, as far as the American people's side of it. He understands our people well enough. I have relied on him before for research; he understands how to do it. Thanks for your part in the book project—I appreciate that.

In addition to Dr. Kersey, I needed help from someone to edit the material and provide insight. Deborah S. Yescas gave me lots of help by reviewing the material with me, checking for mistakes, making corrections and revisions, and putting the material in the right places. I deeply appreciate her assistance.

I spoke to Dorothy Downs after speaking with Dr. Kersey because she had been working with me on the book project when I first started. I talked with her about the book and material and seeking assistance from Dr. Kersey. She thought it would take too much time and she was very busy; she said that I had a better choice, and it was a good idea to work with Dr. Kersey. I do appreciate the help she gave me. It kept me going.

When I first started talking about publishing an autobiography, Mayor Stephen E. Clark and the Dade County commissioners were interested in having something like that. They helped me find the funds and resources and supported my project. I appreciate their contribution and the relationship we established with Mayor Clark and the commissioners in office during that time.

I want to acknowledge traditional Miccosukees living in the 1950s and early 1960s, all of whom were involved in the conception and development of the Miccosukee Tribe. They were people with strong traditional beliefs and some with strong spiritual medicine. Some men came from Lake Okeechobee area, although most of them were from our area, which covered Everglades City, West Coast area, Big Cypress Swamp, and the Everglades area. I want to recognize Ingraham Billie, who was a spiritual leader and Miccosukee medicine man from this area; Sam Jones was a spiritual leader, a Creek from Lake Okeechobee; and Oscar Holt was also a Creek spiritual leader. All the rest were traditional people living in our area: Charlie Billie, Willie Jim, Jimmie Billie, Tom Buster, John Poole, Jimmy Tiger, Small Pox Tommie, Frank Willie, Tiger Tiger, Jessie Willie, Sam Willie. These people I want to thank. They were the ones teaching me. They taught me culture, respect, traditional life, and to protect our lives. They were the enduring force behind the recognition of the Miccosukee Tribe and our freedom to exercise our cultural religion and live freely in our beloved homeland. These men have since passed away, but it was their determination to preserve their culture and claim to their homeland that we built our tribal foundation on.

Before we were recognized, we got help from a family of doctors, Dr. Reintz and his sons. Dr. Reintz, the father, was a friend of the Miccosukees. He lived in Allapatah. Our people came to his office to get health care. He used to go hunting in the glades with Miccosukees during the 1930s. Years later, his surviving son, Dr. Billy Reintz, took over and continued giving health care as his father did. He is a friend of the Miccosukees and understands Miccosukees. He helped us by contacting hospitals and setting up services for us.

In the beginning when I was spokesman, I started working with Homer Kimbral, an attorney from Miami. He was helping us on his own time. He was real nice, an older gentleman. I got to know him; he's a fine gentleman. He did promise me he would help Miccosukee people. After we organized, the Bureau of Indian Affairs approved an attorney's contract with Homer Kimbral so he could work with us legally.

LaVerne Madigan of the American Association on Indian Affairs worked with us in the beginning as well. She and her staff helped Indians in the United States. They recognized that we needed help; they had a lot of contacts with the BIA. They knew how to help Indians organize to gain federal recognition. She got killed while negotiating for us with the BIA. Bill Byler took over and finished up. The AAIA is a big organization that helps any tribe in Indian Country.

We appreciated the Women's Club for donating school clothes to our children. After federal recognition we established a portable school. Dade County gave us a portable building to start a school, and the Women's Club supported us by donating clothes and shoes and helped set up funds for education.

I appreciate the work done for the tribe by tribal attorney Bobo Dean. He was a young man when he first started working with us. He worked with a Washington law firm specializing in Indian law. As a new federally recognized tribe, we went through hard times. We enjoyed the accomplishments and happy times too. Mr. Bobo Dean continues to give support and assistance to the Miccosukee Tribe.

BUFFALO TIGER

This book would not have been completed without the generous support and cooperation of many individuals and institutions. The Miccosukee Tribal Council and Chairman Billy Cypress encouraged the project and graciously allowed access to their files, as did the law firm of Hobbs, Straus, Dean and Walker in Washington DC. A partner in that firm, S. Bobo Dean, who represented the American Association on Indian Affairs, as well as Buffalo Tiger and the Miccosukee people for more than thirty years, provided many valuable interpretations of legal and political issues affecting the tribe. A highly respected commentator on national Indian issues, he was also able to offer a cogent assessment of Buffalo Tiger's significance among Native American leaders in the late twentieth century. Julian Pleasants, director of the Samuel Proctor Oral History Program at the University of Florida, rendered an invaluable service by coordinating the transcription and cataloging of all taped interviews, as well as providing access to the center's extensive collection of past interviews with Florida Indians and those associated with them. Research at the National Archives and other collections in the nation's capital was underwritten in part by a 1998 Scholar/Humanist Fellowship from the Florida Humanities Council and a Research Initiation Grant from the Division of Sponsored Research at Florida Atlantic University

Additional valuable support was received from the staff at the National Archives and at Washington National Records Center, Suitland, Maryland. Librarians at both the University of Florida and Florida Atlantic University also offered advice and assistance at crucial stages in the manuscript's development. Several of my colleagues in the History Department at Florida Atlantic University read portions of the manuscript and offered numerous suggestions that greatly improved the final product. Research associate Shelly Lippiello produced a tightly focused study of American Indian autobiography that significantly informed my understanding of the field and helped shape our approach to this narrative. Deborah Yescas, a close relative of Buffalo Tiger, played a vital role in compiling and editing his monologue tapes; she also provided an insightful second Indian perspective during the collaborative editing process. Much of the material contained in the introduction and afterword first appeared in my book *An Assumption of Sovereignty: Social and Political Transformation among the Florida Seminoles, 1953–1979* and is adapted here by permission of the University of Nebraska Press. The research and preparation of a book manuscript inevitably takes its toll on domestic tranquility, no matter how often the routine has been replicated. Nevertheless, as has been the case for so many years, this project received both constant encouragement and incisive criticism from my wife, Ruth Dyer Kersey. Her eagerness to see the story told fully and expeditiously was surpassed only by that of Buffalo Tiger himself. I hope both will be pleased with the outcome.

HARRY A. KERSEY JR.

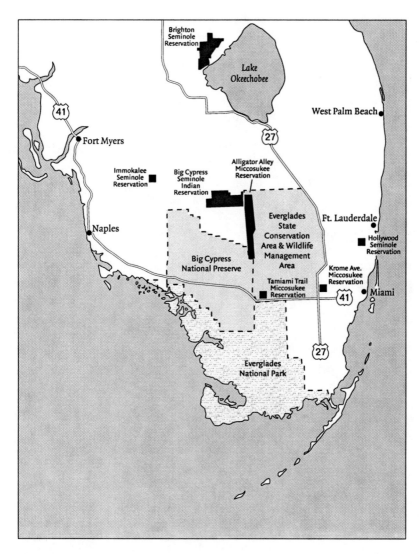

Miccosukee Lands in Florida

INTRODUCTION

Harry A. Kersey Jr.

The Florida Everglades in summer can be a truly hellish place. By midday a blinding laser-beam sun penetrates the cloudless June sky, sending temperatures soaring, while oppressively high humidity becomes a smothering blanket that renders breathing difficult. Traveling is made bearable only by the constant blast of wind created as our airboat skims along a water trail through the tall sawgrass, the roar of its huge Cadillac engine occasionally scattering numerous somnolent turtles and gators from their sunning spots among the matted vegetation. Whenever the craft slows to make sweeping turns that are little more than controlled slides across the shallow water, swarms of gnats, mosquitoes, and other unidentified entomoids previously sucked into the propeller's slipstream impact with an audible *splat* and stick to our perspiration-soaked clothing and skin. I soon find myself inadvertently squinting through dark sunglasses against the water's shimmering glare. Even for those of us who were reared in Florida and actually relish its sultry climate, the Everglades environment can present a grim challenge.

None of this, however, fazes Buffalo Tiger. Perched on his driver's seat a few feet above us, ears muffled against the engine's deafening noise, the Miccosukee Indian elder appears impervious to all elements as he maneuvers our airboat across a seemingly trackless expanse. But it isn't impenetrable to Buffalo; he has traversed this aqueous labyrinth all his life. We are on our way to a tree island—native Floridians call them hammocks—containing a camp where he and other Miccosukees show visitors how their people used to live out here. Although this particular island is just a few miles from the Tamiami Trail, a narrow ribbon of highway that crosses the Everglades between Miami and Naples, only the Indians or highly experienced guides can find it among the maze of vegetation.

On the far western horizon a towering cumulus buildup over the Gulf of Mexico promises an eventual downpour—but probably not today, judging by the light easterly breeze that has come in fitful little gusts all morning. By afternoon the onshore winds will stiffen, keeping the rain clouds out over the gulf. The water level in the Glades is unusually low, accentuating the seven-foot height of the jagged sawgrass and exposing great mats of decaying vegetation. Dozens of wading birds, mostly Purple Gallinules with their outsized feet and brilliant reddish beaks, scuttle about on the lily pads feasting on trapped fingerlings. June is normally well into the wet season, but in recent years the hydrological cycle of south Florida appears to be out of kilter, only to be exacerbated by the El Niño effect. Six months earlier the small island we are approaching had been nearly submerged by the heaviest winter rains in a century, its thatched-roof village structures collapsing into the water lapping around their foundation posts, and the resident raccoon population near starvation except for loaves of day-old Cuban bread provided by Indian guides when they brought tourists. Now the water management officials are releasing millions of gallons to replenish a parched Everglades National Park several miles to the south. If the water level continues to drop, it will soon be impossible to run the airboats.

This last wild stretch of Everglades, some two hundred thousand acres, has become in effect little more than a water impoundment area for coastal cities and a tightly controlled drainage for agricultural interests. The Miccosukee Tribe, although legally a perpetual lessee within the conservation area, has no effective control over water allocation policy even in its own territory. Tribal attorneys have filed numerous suits against both state and federal authorities for polluting the Everglades. The sawgrass that covers 60 to 70 percent of the region—it is actually a sedge named *Cladium jamaicensis*—is being infiltrated, and in places overrun, by cattails and other non-native plants because of nutrient runoff from farms and groves. Mercury contamination in the Everglades waters and fish taken from them has reached alarming levels, but government agencies fail to take effective action. They only issue warnings not to eat the fish.

The airboat engine is killed, and we drift slowly toward a small makeshift landing consisting of cypress poles and planking. The island's raccoon population eagerly comes out to greet us, their expressive bandit-masked faces and elegant paws silently imploring us for food. We cannot resist throwing chunks of bread to the castaways.

"The Everglades are dying," declares Buffalo Tiger. "The land cannot recover from this. Water used to be clean, used to be lots of fish, lots of snakes, lots of birds. Indian life used to be easy because you only knew one life; it belonged to you; it belonged to our people. You learned your language, you know your village, you know what you're going to do, you know what daddy and mama and your uncle and grandmother taught you. But today it's not like that." It is a flat, amazingly unemotional statement of fact coming from someone whose eight decades have been spent here and who epitomizes the struggle to save the land and heritage of his people.

Tiger is tall for a Florida Indian, a lean man whose physical appearance belies his years. Only streaks of gray in thick dark hair, and weather-beaten lines at the corners of his eyes, mark him as a tribal elder. He speaks softly and articulately in slightly halting, slowly cadenced English. Although his grammar reveals a lack of formal schooling, it never detracts from the message. Like other Indians of his age, Tiger views present conditions as intimately bound with the past. From an indigenous perspective, history is cyclical rather than linear. One cannot understand what things should be cherished today without understanding what was meaningful to the Miccosukee people in the past, what has always been valuable. His arm makes a sweeping gesture as he continues, "When I was a boy, this land was wet all the time. The fish, and turtles, and alligators always here. Now we can never be sure."

It is not difficult to understand his concern. The constant whipsawing between flood and drought conditions, sometimes dictated by nature but more often the result of conflicting state and federal water management policies, has taken a devastating toll on the Everglades in the last fifty years, particularly its bird and animal life. Today an array of competing interests—federal, state, and municipal governments, agribusiness, and environmentalists, to name but a few—are struggling to dictate an agenda for the remaining Everglades. One major voice has so far not been accorded a full hearing: that of the only people who still live there, the Miccosukees and, a bit farther north, their relatives the Seminoles.

Buffalo Tiger has seen the Everglades and the culture of his people undergo profound transformations. As a youngster growing up in a traditional Miccosukee Indian camp he was taught to respect medicine men and tribal elders, spoke only the Native language, and learned to fish, hunt, and trap the abundant wildlife. Above all, he was taught to respect the land, which was his people's home and source of livelihood. Although his family kept a permanent camp on the east side of the Everglades, they moved about freely during hunting season. From the family and clan relatives he also learned the religious rituals and beliefs that bound his people together. The central element was a traditional busk, or fasting, ceremony known as the Green Corn Dance, which, in addition to celebrating the Miccosukees' belief in their supreme spiritual power, Breathmaker, revitalized their identity as a people. The traditional council of elders and medicine men who presided over the Green Corn Dance was the only semblance of government that the widely scattered Miccosukee families recognized.

All Indians in Florida were called Seminoles until the 1940s, and the federal government considered them a single tribe, but they actually belonged to two distinct linguistic groups: one spoke Miccosukee and the other Creek. These languages stem from the same Muskogean language family but are mutually unintelligible, although many Florida Indians have learned to converse in both. Unlike the Creek speakers who lived north of Lake Okeechobee, the very traditional Miccosukee people, who call themselves *Eelaponke*, "the People," wanted as little as possible to do with the white settlers who moved into southern Florida in increasing numbers early in this century. Trading with whites was one thing, but adopting their language and lifestyle was out of the question. Thus when the more acculturated Seminoles relocated to government reservations in the 1920s and 1930s, took up cattle raising, sent their children to school, and began working for the Bureau of Indian Affairs, the Miccosukees remained sequestered in their Everglades camps. By the 1940s a large group of Miccosukees, for their own political reasons, also chose to accept reservation life and later became part of the Seminole Tribe. This exodus left a core of some three hundred people who chose to follow the traditional ways of their ancestors.

In time, the Miccosukees who lived near the Tamiami Trail found it necessary to communicate with state and federal officials on a variety of issues concerning their political and economic welfare. Since few of the elders spoke English, much less could read or write it, they turned to Buffalo Tiger to represent them to outsiders. He was one of only a few young Miccosukee men who had extensive experience in both worlds.

Although he is a man who moves easily in white and Indian cultures, when it comes to values Buffalo Tiger is a confirmed traditionalist who feels strongly that too much of his people's distinct folk knowledge is being lost in the rush to adopt modern ways. Miccosukees, he claims, must know who they are, where they came from, and what they believe if they are to survive as a unique people. In recounting the details of his own rich life, which has spanned most of the twentieth century, Tiger incorporates the essential elements of what it means to be Indian, traditions he learned as a youngster. Without that knowledge, he fears, the current generation will lose its value system, religious beliefs, and perhaps individual liberties. In his view Indians' personal freedoms are intertwined with their land rights, and both are constantly under attack from outside forces that would limit the people's traditional rights to hunt, fish, maintain camps, and observe religious ceremonies in the Everglades and to administer tribal justice. Members of the younger generation must retain this knowledge if they are to sustain their rights. In part that is why, at an age when most Indian elders are content to quietly tend the fires of memory, he is vigorously engaged in the preparation of this life history as a lasting legacy to the Miccosukee people. It is an effort to share accumulated wisdom about many things, some now only dimly remembered, long after he and others of his generation are gone. His story should also provide a source of pride in what the modern Miccosukee Tribe accomplished in its first quarter century under his leadership, achievements that paved the way for its current success as a sovereign Indian nation.

The Miccosukees and Their History

The Native peoples called Seminoles and Miccosukees are not indigenous to Florida. They were once part of the Muskogee/Creek nation of Georgia and Alabama; in the eighteenth century they migrated to Spanish Territory, perhaps contacting remnants of earlier peninsular groups. At its height the Muskogee domain encompassed territory between the Piedmont and Gulf of Mexico and extended from the Black Warrior/Tombigbee watershed of Alabama to the Savannah River in Georgia.[1] Although there was a great diversity of tribal and linguistic groups in this region, about three-quarters of the people spoke a language in the Muskogean linguistic family and thus identified themselves as Muskogees.[2] Initially lacking any form of central government, the Muskogees lived in some sixty independent towns with their own political and war chiefs. Each of these towns, known as *talwas*, was a major ceremonial center with a square ground, the sacred precinct at the heart of Muskogee social and religious experience. Every square-ground town along with its satellite villages comprised an independent tribal polity.[3]

The Muskogees were loosely united by patterns of social and political organization as well as religious beliefs. Exogamous matrilineal clans were the most important of these elements. Each *talwa* was made up of extended families belonging to the various clans. Clans reckoned descent from a common ancestor, and membership was determined through the female lineage.[4] The clan system established an individual's personal identity, defined social and political roles, and maintained stable social order throughout the Creek nation. Indians were reluctant to attack individuals from other clans for fear of provoking vengeance. As the Muskogee population grew, clans also facilitated the assimilation of newcomers, since membership defined individual identity across tribal lines: all members of the same clan were related regardless of their political affiliation.

The clans were matrilocal as well as matrilineal. A married woman and her family went to live in the camp of her mother, surrounded by clan-related females and their families. These related families were basic units of residence and social interaction known as *huti* and served as the primary vehicle for informal instruction of the young.[5] All knowledge relating to clan origins, functions, and ritual roles was transmitted to the child through the mother and her relatives, primarily the clan uncles. Women owned the homestead, household goods, and means of production. The locus of women's power in Creek society was found in the home, child rearing, and cultivation of food.[6] The men's sphere was distinctly different, focusing on town political life, hunting, and relationships with outsiders as traders and warriors.

Muskogees held a common set of cosmological beliefs, or worldview.[7] Their supreme being was Breathmaker, who brought order to the universe. The Muskogees' most sacred space was the square ground, and their most respected ceremony was an annual busk ritual known as the Green Corn Dance, which honored Breathmaker by giving thanks for his gifts, exemplified by the new crop of green corn. The ceremony was also a time for spiritual and social revitalization of the people. Old fires were extinguished, and a period of personal purification was observed. A court session of elders judged transgressors, and young men coming of age received their adult names. Ritually, the kindling of a new fire on the square ground during the final day symbolized resolution of conflict between the clans and the people as a whole. For this reason women, who represented fertility and the perpetuation of individual lineages, were not allowed on the square ground until the conclusion of the busk ceremony, when they took new fire to their homes. This act metaphorically reaffirmed the dominance of the group over individual clans.[8]

The name "Creeks" was originally associated with a small tribal group, the Ochese, first contacted by whites on a Georgia creek in the late 1600s. "Ochese Creeks" was later shortened to "Creeks" and applied by English traders to all Muskogee peoples. The Creeks were geographically divided into two groups: the towns on the Alabama, Coosa, and Tallapoosa Rivers were called Upper Creeks, and those along the Chattahoochee and Flint Rivers were Lower Creeks.[9] Muskogee was the internal language of most Creek towns and the lingua franca between towns. But in a large number of Lower Towns the internal language was Hitchiti, a language in the same family but not mutually intelligible with Muskogee. A town called Mikasuki was one of those Hitchiti-speaking Lower Creek enclaves, and eventually Hitchiti and Mikasuki became synonymous.

By 1715, after a series of disastrous colonial Indian wars on the southern frontier, the Creeks withdrew to their lands in western Georgia near the Chattahoochee River. At the same time, a number of Lower Towns were enticed to remove to an unpopulated region in Spanish Florida, filling a demographic void created by English raids that destroyed the Spanish mission Indians between 1704 and 1710. There they could escape both constant pressures from English settlers and political domination by Upper Creeks. Over time expatriate Creeks led by a chief named Cowkeeper moved onto the Alachua prairies east of the Suwanee River while Mikasukis under Secofee settled westward in the area of present-day Tallahassee.[10] A second Mikasuki group headed by King Philip which settled east of the St. Johns River was connected by marriage with the Cowkeeper band.

The Creeks derisively called their people who had migrated to Spanish Florida simano-li, a term borrowed from the Spanish word cimarrón, meaning "wild or runaway."[11] Over the years this term was transformed into Seminole, and after several Upper Creek towns migrated to Florida, the dominant language became Muskogee. The Mikasukis never lost their language and separate identity within the larger Seminole polity, however. There are two variant spellings of the ethnonym *Mikasuki* in the literature. Historically, the preferred anthropological-linguistic usage has been *Mikasuki*, applied to both the tribal group and its form of the Hitchiti language. Until this century only a lake near Tallahassee in north Florida bore the spelling *Miccosukee*. When the modern Miccosukee Tribe of Indians of Florida was organized in 1962, it adopted that spelling.

The Seminoles and Miccosukees made substantial adaptations to the environmental conditions and subsistence patterns of north Florida, but they kept most essential elements of Creek culture, although some persisted in attenuated form. Even though population centers were smaller and more dispersed than in the Creek nation, towns in north Florida retained the square ground as a center of political and religious activities, and family, clan, and kinship patterns remained of prime importance. By the time of the American Revolution these immigrants were well settled in their Florida lands and controlled a large number of African escapees from plantations in Georgia and the Carolinas. This control was not the type of chattel slavery practiced by other southeastern tribes such as the Cherokees and Creeks, however. These so-called Seminole Negroes occupied their own villages, paid fealty to the Seminoles, and occasionally married into Indian lineages; they also became staunch military allies of the Indians in resisting pressures from the United States after it gained control of the peninsula from Spain in 1821.[12]

Despite an 1823 federal treaty guaranteeing the Seminoles a Florida reservation and annuities for twenty years, the threat posed by free blacks among the Indians, as well as the settlers' insatiable appetite for land, led the territorial government to demand the immediate removal of the Seminoles. Congress assisted with the 1830 Indian Removal Act, which required all eastern tribes to relocate west of the Mississippi River. It also resulted in a combined Seminole/Miccosukee resistance known as the Second Seminole War (1835–42).[13] After seven years of guerrilla-style warfare costing millions of dollars and thousands of lives on both sides, fewer than one thousand Indians remained in Florida. The Third Seminole War (1855–58) further reduced this number to around three hundred persons, the ancestors of today's Seminole and Miccosukee tribes.

In the aftermath of these wars the old patterns of Indian life in Florida were thoroughly disrupted. Moreover, the great majority of Indians remaining in Florida were Miccosukees. The square-ground towns, extensive fields, and cattle herds they had known in north Florida were abandoned, and the people gathered in regional concentrations near Lake Okeechobee or deep in the Everglades.[14] Around 1900 these large communities broke up, and smaller extended family camps were established.[15] These camps—headed by a *posi*, or "grandmother"—provided a stable setting for child rearing and a nexus of psychological support, social interaction, and physical protection. This stability was especially important because Seminole marriages were fragile, owing to the risk of death or captivity that men faced in warfare and hunting, as well as the nonbinding marriage bond, which could be dissolved at the next Green Corn Dance. Anthropologist Brent Weisman has concluded that Creek matrilineal *huti* were the cultural antecedents of the Seminole/Miccosukee camps during the nineteenth century.[16] Women came to outnumber men in the remnant Indian population. In an 1880 study for the Bureau of Ethnology, Clay MacCauley found just 208 Seminoles in Florida, with significantly more female than male adults, although this ratio was reversed among youngsters.[17]

The annual Green Corn Dance was retained, but traditional patterns of social and political organization were altered to meet the needs of a greatly reduced population. The medicine men, keepers of the spiritually powerful medicine bundles, emerged as both political and religious leaders of the people, and activities associated with the medicine bundle became the focus of corporate devotion at the busk ceremony. Once a year the scattered camps came together for this ritual, which still served as a time for personal spiritual renewal and communal revitalization. Although many Indian leaders had died or moved west as a result of the wars, the remaining medicine men and elders conveyed essential elements of the Miccosukee worldview to succeeding generations. Stripped of many elaborations and devoid of some nuances found in nineteenth-century Muskogee cosmology, the message of Breathmaker nevertheless remained at the core of Miccosukee beliefs.

Most Miccosukees settled on tree islands in the Everglades called hammocks; the Seminoles remained in the scrub and pinelands north of Lake Okeechobee. Again, they made a series of ethnoecologic adaptations to ensure survival. New forms of clothing, housing, transportation, and subsistence evolved to meet the dictates of climate and terrain. The log structures of north Florida were replaced by elevated, open-sided, thatched-roof *chickees;* dugout canoes were used to traverse the Everglades and Lake Okeechobee. Lightweight and loose-fitting clothing was more practical than the buckskins and leggings worn in north Florida.[18] In the camps Miccosukees retained gender-specific economic roles.[19] Women were responsible for the home, child rearing, tending the family garden, and caring for animals; they also harvested and prepared the wild *Zamia* root used to make *coontie* starch. Men were responsible for building the thatched-roof *chickees* and clearing the ground for gardens; they also contributed to the family subsistence by hunting and fishing, cutting the huge cypress trees used to fashion dugout canoes, and trapping and trading for a market economy.

In the late 1870s Seminole men began an intensive commerce in otter pelts, bird plumes, and alligator hides.[20] These commodities were valuable to the international fashion industry, which converted them into alligator shoes, belts, and luggage; fur collars for coats; and feathered millinery. Indians did not trade in the literal sense of barter; rather, they engaged in cash transactions for their goods and used the income to purchase goods sold by white storekeepers. By the turn of the twentieth century Seminole material culture showed great dependence on store-bought goods such as iron tools, bolts of cloth, and hand-powered sewing machines. Cooking methods and diet changed as the Seminoles added canned goods, coffee, and tea and substituted milled grits for native *coontie* flour in preparing the staple food *sofkee,* or corn gruel. Men discarded antiquated weapons and bought modern guns and traps to improve their hunting.

As Indian men changed their economic goals from subsistence to commerce in this period, the reciprocity of gender roles shifted as well.[21] Men spent longer periods of time away from home, and women assumed more responsibility for daily decision making. At the same time, nuclear family units began to leave the extended family camps and became widely dispersed across south Florida.[22] In a reconfiguration of clan support mechanisms, women continued to rear the family but enjoyed less constant interaction and support from their clan relatives. Women played a limited part in the economic transactions at the trading posts, preferring to stay in the background and convey their wishes through the men. As a result it was Indian men who developed some facility with English to transact business. During the trading period Indian women assumed the role of cultural conservators in language as well as customs of dress and deportment.

The Florida East Coast Railway arrived at Miami in 1896, and as settlements spread throughout south Florida intercultural contacts with Indians increased. Indian women began to take a more active economic role, selling their baskets, buckskin moccasins, braided belts, and alligator teeth necklaces. The production and sale of elegant Seminole patchwork goods to tourists began around the time of World War I.[23] Early in the twentieth century, however, a number of factors led to the collapse of the Indians' mainstay hunting-trapping economy. After the railroad came, there was a rapid expansion of groves and farms, forcing Indians from many of their traditional hunting grounds and campsites near the East Coast. After 1905 the state of Florida embarked on a grand scheme to systematically drain the Everglades for agricultural development.[24] Canals dug from Lake Okeechobee to Miami lowered the Everglades' water table, leading to a drastic decline in the wildlife population. The final blow was the outbreak of World War I, which cut off European markets for the commodities the Indians provided.

Born in 1920, Buffalo Tiger grew up during a decades-long transitional period. The Indians responded to the changes around them in two ways: some retained their traditional practices, and others were willing to accept a degree of assimilation by working for wages and adopting reservation life.

A MICCOSUKEE CHILDHOOD

Early in the twentieth century the lifestyle of Miccosukee Indians living in the Florida Everglades had changed very little since the late 1800s. They maintained their *chickee* camps and small gardens on widely scattered tree islands, or hammocks. They practiced a gender-based division of labor. Indian men fished, hunted, and trapped wildlife for food and sold the hides to white traders in nearby towns. Miccosukee women were in charge of the camp, where they tended to the cooking, sewing, child rearing, and myriad other everyday chores. The Miccosukees strictly observed the matrilineal clan system. They were also matrilocal: women of the same clan lived with their families in a camp headed by the senior clan matron. The Green Corn Dance remained the central religious ritual of the people, and the white man's religions had made no inroads. Except for occasional visits to Miami, the Miccosukees had limited interaction with the outside world until the Tamiami Trail opened in the 1920s. It was in such a camp setting, surrounded by his relatives, that young Buffalo Tiger was introduced to the culture and beliefs of his people. In this chapter he describes what it was like to grow up Miccosukee.

The Camp

People call me Buffalo Tiger. My birthday is March 6, 1920. I was born in a little village; we called it Grandfather's village, and we lived there a long time. We called it Grandfather's village, but it was really Grandmother's village. In our customs we have to believe the wife is always the boss over the camps and families—so the grandmother, she is the big boss! My grandmother, we called her *Posi*, and that's all we ever called her because we did not know and did not say the real name. It is a custom of Miccosukees not to call elder people by their names. So we called her *Posi* and she was boss of the village.

My mother was of the same clan, the Bird clan. I can call her by her English name, Sally Tiger.

My grandfather was of the Big City clan; sometimes people call them the Frogs. His name was Charlie Willie. My grandmother and grandfather, they were pretty old.

My daddy was from the Otter clan. His name was Tiger Tiger.

I had about ten people in my family. My older brother people called Jimmy Tiger. The girl after him passed away years ago when she was young. I do not remember her name. Another sister was born after her; her name was Mickey. She got married, but she passed away. I was born after her. I have a brother who was born after me, about a year and a half later. We called him Josie; he has passed away. The other brother I have is younger than him. His name is Tommy Tiger; his nickname is "Cokie." Then a girl was born after him; her name is Annie. She got married and was renamed Annie Jim; she's still living pretty well with her husband. Then another girl was born; we called her Lois. She has passed away. A younger boy was born; his name was Bobby Tiger, and he got to be an alligator wrestler, but he has passed away. The youngest sister was born; her name was Mary. She got married and became Mary Osceola. She has passed away.

I cannot remember everything that happened at that particular day and time. But I began to realize I was living in a camp. This happened to be in the Glades. I began to see things and realize what I heard. I felt so wonderful during those times. I can see my grandfather wearing traditional clothes and a hat the medicine men used to wear. He looked scary to me. I remember seeing him at his camp and seeing my grandmother at that

Fig. 1. Miccosukee children at Musa Isle Village, ca. 1925. Buffalo Tiger is at left in top row. His grandfather, Charlie Willie, stands next to him. His uncle Frank Willie is on the right of the picture. Courtesy of the Seminole/Miccosukee Photographic Archive, Ft. Lauderdale FL.

camp. She always seemed to be around the fire cooking something or boiling *sofkee* made from corn. We always managed to drink that.

I remember seeing my mother around the cooking *chickee*. I remember seeing another lady; she was an aunt of mine. I can't remember seeing other children my age to play with.

One afternoon at that particular time, I remember clearly the birds making noise. Beautiful red birds, the cardinals, sitting up on top of the trees. There was a tree standing there, and they were sitting up there singing and singing. I kept looking at them so red, so beautiful. I thought—I remember that clearly—how does the bird make noise?

It happened that same afternoon the wind was blowing from the southwest. It was blowing hard, and clouds were moving. At that particular time

I was feeling very good. I got all excited because the wind was blowing and the clouds were coming closer to us. That made me feel so good. It was getting ready to rain. I had a little bow and arrow my dad made for me. I picked it up and was running and jumping because the wind made me feel so wonderful. I took this bow and arrow and shot it against the wind. The wind was strong enough to carry my arrow back to camp. It finally hit my grandfather and almost hit his eye, but it did not—it hit his head. I could not say anything. They did not realize I did not shoot him; I had shot up in the air against the wind, but the arrow came down because the wind was blowing hard. So it hit my grandfather, and it made him bleed. I did not feel good. My grandmother and mother blamed me that I shot and hit him. I was trying to tell them I did not. So I got whipped for that. But I did not feel bad because I did not shoot him, and I did not want to hurt him, but it happened. They never believed me; my mother, my grandmother, and my grandfather all did not believe me. But I was not feeling hurt. They whipped me and told me never to do that again. I didn't accept that because I didn't do it. I was just having fun and enjoying what nature was doing to me, I thought. But I did not know what nature was about at that time.

I remember that particular camp because my grandfather had a type of store, kind of like a grocery store. It was made out of wood frame. They had a bunch of groceries inside, and he traded with our people. Anything he could sell he bought, or he traded for groceries. Then he brought them into the city, Miami. I do not know where. He sold whatever he brought to the people he knew. Then he got a little money to buy groceries and material things and take them back out there to sell to our people. They did not have to come into town for anything; they bought from him. I do not think he spoke any English, but he managed to handle money pretty well. He sold shotguns; he sold traps for animals; he sold about everything he could to the people. A lot of Miccosukee people knew that, so they came from all over to see him and trade with him. Meantime he let them have credit, so people had someplace they could go and get things they needed; then they would go back. In a way we were lucky with our grandparents because we learned so much at that time, but we didn't realize that was the business they were doing. Many Miccosukee people came and traded with him and took groceries home with them because they brought in all types of hides: otter skin, raccoon skin, alligator skin. They were worth good money at that time, I suppose. I really did not know the business. But I know that's the kind of thing he was doing. And we wanted to go in the store so many times because he had cookies. We'd go in there—he let us in sometimes and gave us pieces of cookie. We'd come out and eat them. It was hard to get in the store because he would keep us away, but we did not mind that.

I remember that the boat dock area was north of the camp. Always Miccosukee men were coming in with a canoe and spent a day or two and got what they wanted and went away from there. I don't know their names, and I don't know who they were; but those activities were like that. Sometimes we had about three or four families in that little village; all seemed to be kin. Then other kids came from different places, and we always had a lot of youngsters to play with. Other clans could live with us a while because they had their own village. They were just coming in to pick up different things and go back. I also remember my dad would go out in the canoe and come back with lots of corn, pumpkins, and potatoes for us to eat. We had an outdoor table made just for that. It was built outdoors and was big enough for the corn, pumpkins, potatoes, and whatever we wanted to put in the sun. We put them out on the table and let the sun hit them a few days, a few weeks. We thought that made them sweeter. We always did that; my dad, my mother, my grandmother, we always did that.

There were all kinds of fish; all kinds of birds; all kinds of snakes; all kinds of game. There were just too many sometimes.

I remember my brothers and cousins; we took a canoe out, and we always managed to get fish. Sometimes in deeper water there were lots of fish; we just rocked the boat, and fish started jumping all over the place and they got in our canoe. We took them [back], and our mothers and grandmothers cooked for us. Turtles—we call them yokche—were not a problem because there were so many at that particular camp.

There was just so much you could learn—like going to bed at night. When we had to go to bed at night, most of the time we washed our feet—we ran around barefoot all day. We had to fix our beds. I grew up sleeping on a hardwood [platform]; we called it the sleeping place. The blanket goes on the hardwood, and a mosquito net comes down and goes over you. I remember at night we all slept in one chickee. Chickees are made from palmetto and cypress frames. Sometimes we built them a pretty good size and sometimes a small size. The family chickee is usually a good size. Children slept in the same place as my dad and mom. We all slept in the same chickee, but the platforms were different. But I was small enough and young enough, so they left me with my dad and mother, and my brothers were there, too. We were small and afraid of night.

During [one particular] night I was afraid. I thought I saw something. I never knew what it was that did that to me. We were sleeping inside a mosquito net. We always used a kerosene lamp; it gave us light. It was cut down so just a very little light was coming out, and you could see a shadow. I thought I saw something moving back and forth. Our heads were facing toward the east. That's what we learned to do; we always faced that way. I looked down at my foot; it was facing toward the west. I could see the little light and something moving back and forth, and I got real afraid and did not say anything. It just kept moving back and forth. I wondered what it was. I thought maybe somebody was walking back and forth; I saw that, I thought.

But there was nobody there. No noise, nothing.

It did that maybe twenty minutes and managed to go away. But I never told my mom and dad that. I was just so afraid I couldn't sleep that night. I never told anybody what I saw, things moving, because I had no idea what it was. But I know I was afraid.

We were told night is not a time for us to play. Night is a time we should behave and sit and listen to stories. Do what you must do and sit around the fire. Sometimes you lay on the table under the *chickee*, facing the sky, looking at the sky, sometimes the stars. Nighttime stories would be told to you. We always did these things. So they told us, our parents told us, we should never run and never go places at night because night is not a time for us to play and run and be happy. Spirits from the body must enjoy the night, so we should let them enjoy the night. And our people enjoy living during daytime. So maybe that was bothering me that time. I did not ever find out what that light was.

Many things happened to us, but nothing serious; no big problems. We just had to know where we would be going hunting next time. We did a lot of hunting. Sometimes in fall, sometimes spring; it depended on what type of game we were going to be hunting. I was too young to know what I should learn that particular time. They had not taught me anything yet. I remember many Miccosukee men coming in with guns. They had all kinds of guns and must have had them for years and years. They showed them to us—my brothers, my cousins, us boys together. They showed us, and they told us which ones were used for each type of game, and they showed us the type the soldiers used to kill people with. Also, I remember seeing the gun that you have to make a bullet for, and it had a big barrel for the powder because they had to make their own bullet and use the powder to make it blow.

We lived there for a long time, I guess, but I can't remember. As far as the Tamiami Trail—it did not go all the way through. It went as far as where we were in my grandmother and grandfather's camp. Maybe half a mile northwest the Tamiami Trail ended.

We visited other places in the Glades where Miccosukee people lived. Our people identified the different villages by giving them names like "Crying over Land" or "High Place." To me it was a beautiful place. There was lots of water, and we traveled back and forth in the canoe to visit these places. Most all Miccosukee camps have bunches of bananas and sugarcane, pumpkins, potatoes, and things like that. So us boys visited other camps like our aunts', or maybe other folks that lived nearby us. We spent time chewing sugarcane; sometimes people had bananas, and we enjoyed eating them. In between times we did a lot of swimming because the water looked so good. It looked so clean you could see the bottom. You could see fish, all kinds of fish.

I myself enjoyed watching fish. Sometimes we lay in the canoe with nothing to do but enjoy watching little fish in the water. Way down in the water the big freshwater shrimp were there. They have small holes in the muck, and they go in there. When they want food they come out and get their food and go back in. But there were a lot of freshwater shrimp and lots of little shrimp swimming underwater. We used to watch that. And also there were all kinds of small turtles; we used to watch them too. If you look and wait—you just have to spend a little time just waiting and be patient. They can come out and start swimming and doing things like they were playing with you. That's how we enjoyed watching so many times. I did anyhow; some of the boys didn't like to do that. But I did that so many times because I guess I have imagination. I remember that the water was so clean you could see the bass, big ones and little ones. You could see the mullet that used to be out there. And some are tarpons; we used to see them. But I was too little to get those fish; I could only get them by rocking the boat to let them get in. As far as turtles, it was no problem for us to get them.

We had to learn what we could kill for food. We were taught never to kill anything except what would be good eating, and that's it. The grandmother would tell a young man whatever he sees, go back and tell his grandmother or aunt. The aunt or grandmother would say, "That is a deer that you are talking about. It is edible; if you kill it, I'll cook it for you." And you went hunting and got that deer. The type of bird he saw he told his grandmother or aunt, and she would say, "That's a bird. It is edible; if you kill it, we'll cook it for you." You came back with it, and they cooked it for you. And other times a grandmother or aunt would say, "It's not edible; don't kill it." That's the way it goes. We've been taught what we should eat and what we should not eat and don't destroy and kill it. That's how we had to learn from nighttime stories.

That's how we grew up.

When you are little, being a Miccosukee, you have a clear mind, a very clear mind about what you are. We had no idea about another life, the city life; we just learned and knew ourselves. We were so comfortable with our father and our grandmothers and our people and what they taught us.

We didn't have many toys to play with. I remember when I was a little boy and was old enough to have little pets. Someone gave me white birds. I kept them for a while, and they flew away. Other times they got me ducks; I kept them for a while, but we had to let them go. The toy I always seemed to have was a bow and arrow. We had a toy like a little canoe made out of cypress—not very much, but sometimes I played with it. I enjoyed having them. But mostly what excited me was nature: what I saw, what was around me.

When we were old enough to sit around the fire at night, there were so many things people taught us. I didn't really think people were teaching me at that time. But that's what our mothers, fathers, and grandmothers were doing. But you never think somebody is teaching you. They just make you realize something you should or shouldn't do, and you have to believe in those things. Miccosukees did not have much back then, but we had bedtime stories that were told many times. There were different kinds of stories about animals or birds, reptiles or snakes. There were funny stories about Brer Rabbit, who always tried to pretend to be something else, although he was a rabbit. Stories like that were told at night. Stories were usually told to children while they lay on the tables where they slept. Other times they would just lie on the ground on a blanket. Whoever was telling the story would have them all lie down facing the sky. The stories like Brer

Rabbit were funny, but some stories were sad. Children enjoyed listening to them.

When we were young, all of us were told we could not kill even little spiders. We didn't go around killing what we saw. So even the little spiders—if we killed them we had to sing or say something to explain why we did it. Because our mother and grandmother said you must do that because there are bigger things that will hurt you later if you just kill it and walk away. You must always let them know you did not mean to do that but you did it because of some reason, so the bigger things later won't hurt you. So many times we did not kill little insects or spiders particularly. That part, it seems to be the most beautiful way of seeing things.

Sickness and Medicine

We learned there were so many different kinds of sickness we could get. We used to say only Indians could get sick that way. We picked up major types of sickness; could be from any animal that had sickness. Somehow we didn't have to play with it; we didn't have to touch it; we didn't have to be close by. The sickness just stuck to us because it was in the air. Sometimes little girls and little boys got sick from that.

The adults who could make traditional medicine knew exactly what caused it because of the way the child acted. Sometimes they could tell by looking in the eye; sometimes they saw the hands moving. So they knew exactly what to do for that boy or girl that was sick. They always used their medicine for that. They would tell you what type of material they had to have to make medicine for that particular sick boy or girl. Parents had to know that, too, because the man who is going to make medicine will tell you to go get this particular tree, not the leaf, maybe the bark. For some particular trees you can only use the leaves, maybe four or five different types of roots or trees or plants. Sometimes some were not really plants, just something that would help the children when they were sick. It is hard for me to explain because it's like little mildew or fungus you would find that would be used as medicine for a type of sickness. So the medicine man had to tell you, or a woman could do that. Daddy, Mama, or someone would go ahead and look for it and get everything together, and they made medicine for that particular sickness. The child or boy would get well.

That's what I did. A lady made medicine, and I got better. That is the way it is. Sometimes I got sick from spiders when I was a kid. It didn't have to be bites; could be spiders you were dreaming about. You could be dreaming so many times about that type of spider. Then my brother got sick from a monkey. I was a little boy, but my brother got sick and people quickly made medicine. They told my mom and my daddy he got sick from a monkey and you have to get this type of medicine. You have to go out and find different types of plants. They made medicine for him. He did not have to come into contact with a real monkey. The same goes for me. I didn't have to contact that type of spider; I just got sick. When I got sick, I got fever and just couldn't walk anymore. I was going to die. Good thing this old lady took care of me. She told me she was going to take care of me, that I'm going to get better, and I did. She made medicine for me.

Good medicine people could make the child get better, but only for major types of sickness. Let's say today cholesterol is too high. We call it white man's sickness. Sugar diabetes is another white man's sickness. People used to tell us there will be a time when because of the food we eat and life changes, you will be adopting the white man's illness and our medicine is not going to work so good. So that's the way we are today.

Years ago Indian medicine worked good for us. When we were younger, we had to stay in line, knowing we could get sick if we go too far this way, or too far north, or too far west, or anything like that. We always had to stay in line. It was a little strict. Years ago we were like that. Let's say my mother washed my clothes, put them out in the sun on a tree or some type of clothes hanger, and let them dry. They always told us you bring your clothes in before sundown. After sundown a lot of fog is coming down from the sky with lots of sickness. It'll get into your clothes, and after you wear them you will get sick. So always we had to take our clothes in before sundown when I was growing up. Those are the kinds of things I had to learn.

Boys and Girls

When Miccosukees lived in the Glades, boys had different types of games they played and things they did to enjoy themselves. Families lived together on a small island or hammock, the high dry places in the Florida Everglades. At home they had their own sleeping *chickees* and their own tables to sleep on. There was one eating table and a cooking *chickee*.

Boys learned how to sing songs just for boys. They learned how to sing

Corn Dance songs. There were different dance songs, and they learned the special songs for the different dances. This made it easier for boys to learn songs. You could not be a leader of a dance unless you knew the song that went with it. The dance leader is up front, and he is the one who has to sing. The others fall in place behind him. Everybody sings, but the leader makes a lot of noise and sings so loud so everybody can hear him. The people let him know right away if he makes a mistake while singing. When a fellow is dancing, a young woman usually dances behind him and dances for him. Boys learned to do many of those things at home. Families used to dance in the back yard, and that is how boys learned to sing and to know what the Corn Dance would be like. Girls usually do not sing, and only the best boy singers would get to sing.

Boys and girls used to sit around the fire at night and play a game with the fire. They had a stick they would burn and would make a few marks on the ground. They would mark where they thought the burned stick would fall. Then they started burning little sticks, maybe six or seven inches tall. The stick went round and round until it fell. Sometimes it fell between nobody, or sometimes it fell where someone had made a mark. That was a game the children thought was fun. There were other things they did at night, but when their parents said it was time to go to bed, they did.

Some children had different pets. Some had ducks, a big bird like an egret, or raccoons that were kept as pets when they were babies. When they were babies they were easy to get, but they got mean as they got older and had to be set free. Dogs were popular pets, too. Dog is a friend of a boy and his daddy. The dog is the best thing to have. Not girls—they didn't have dogs.

During the daytime there was always plenty of time to play games and do a little hunting. Alligator, fish, deer, and turkey all have a way to find their food, too. Boys were taught that if they understand how a particular type of bird or animal eats or does things, then they could find them. It was always best to find animals in the morning when it was cool and the sun had just risen, or when it was late enough and everything was calm. Even the eagle and blue heron had certain habits and places to eat. The same goes for alligators. Alligators hang around almost the same area all the time. Once a boy had found where gators stay, he could see them when he wanted to. There always was a routine way of doing things. Once a boy learned that, he knew how a type of bird or animal lived and its habits.

Boys learned how to hunt for deer. There is a certain way of doing that. Little boys might go find a deer, a big buck. They could find them but never could get them because they did not know how. Their fathers or uncles would have to teach them how to kill a deer and bring it home so that when they grew up they could do it.

Boys went into low water in the Glades. They could walk there and look for holes in the muck where freshwater shrimp lived. Freshwater shrimp grew to about three or four inches long. Some were very small, but others were big; their legs were dark brown. Different types of fish build nests and lay their eggs under the water. When they hatched, the mother usually would hang around and look after the little fish. She would protect them.

There used to be a lot of big trees that the boys would climb. They would get together where the birds gathered to spend the night. They knew where to find them on a big hammock and would go there and sit in the bushes to hide until sundown. Then the birds would come back to sleep after spending their day away. Sometimes the boys would scare them, and they would go away and come back later. The mess birds made smelled like fish; they eat fish all day. Snakes like fish, and a lot of snakes were where the birds made their mess. The boys had to be very careful of that because there were plenty of snakes beneath the trees, but they were having fun. They had fun chasing the small birds around the trees and did that every day. They were always imitating the different types of bird sounds. A bunch of little birds would come to where the boys were hiding under the trees. The small birds would get closer and closer. Some boys just loved going into the bushes or under the trees to sit there imitating birds. There were all kinds of birds around to watch.

A lot of boys would get together and sometimes spend time on different islands. They would go to some islands and spend half a day or almost a day eating sugarcane. Other times they would go where the custard apple was in season and ripe. Just a few hammocks had them, but the boys knew where they were, so they would hunt for them and spend a lot of time up in the tree eating them. They learned many things by watching and had so many things to watch. They did not have to go to school in those days, so they did all these things during the day. They would go home, and their mothers would have food ready for them. They would sit down to eat and enjoy lunch.

There were things boys could play with and things they were not supposed to play with. They were scolded and told not to do something but still might do it and would get caught. Sometimes when children would get out of control, their uncle would be called in. Their mother would tell the uncle to whip or scratch the child. Scratching is one thing that is handled differently for babies and little boys and girls. Sometimes little babies were lightly crossed on their hands. Each hand was scratched on the top of the hand. If a boy or girl was acting naughty, adults would take a big bucket of water and pour it on them to scare them. They realized that could happen, so they behaved. Sometimes children were given whippings. Their mother would take a big stick and whip them. She might tell an uncle or the father to whip them. Discipline made the child behave.

A boy's responsibilities were taught to him by men of his clan. A boy must know his clan and how to behave when visiting other clans. He must always be proud of his clan. At birth all children were given a symbolic baby name. My baby name was Mostaki—it was more like a nickname. At the age of fourteen or fifteen each boy received a man's name at the yearly Green Corn Dance. At this event a boy would go without food or sleep for an entire day and night. He spent the day taking medicine and playing ball. He would dance at night but could not sleep. At the end of the night he received his man's name, which he would keep until he died.

Boys must train to be tough and handle all things, such as cold weather. When it is cold in winter, boys should arise before sunrise, take a bath or swim, and then return to the fireplace to get warm. Boys should learn to care for and meet the needs of a family. A boy should learn to be a good hunter. Boys must know how to work the soil and plant food. They should know which soil is good and the best time of year for growing different things.

A boy learned where to find the right wood and building materials to build chickees for his family. A boy knew how to pole a canoe in order to transport his family from one camp to another. Boys learned how to make medicine. A boy learned how to make friends with boys of other clans, play and do things together. Always play by the rules.

Boys learned about weather, could find the direction the wind is blowing, and knew if rain was coming. We live with weather and nature and are not afraid of it. We learned to get along with nature, as it is an important part of our life. We learned we should not be afraid of nature, like wind and lightning, because we are nature's people. Boys learned to understand the sun, moon, and stars.

Boys should be able to identify all plants and trees, to know which ones are poisonous or edible, to know the uses for the wood of each type of tree.

Boys must know that the night is not a time for play. It is a time to tell stories, learn from elders, or sleep. Boys must go to bed early. Sleep with your head pointed toward the east and feet toward the west in order to get up early.

A boy always got permission from elders to entertain himself, such as learning traditional songs and dances.

A boy did not listen to his mother's conversation with another woman. He probably did not know what they talked about. A boy knew that mothers would put their baby in a hammock and swing the baby. Mothers or sisters would sing to their baby. Boys would know that the baby was sleeping when Mother was singing for them.

Families

When a boy was little, he and his brothers and cousins learned from each other, but they mostly learned from their fathers. When a boy got old enough to be helpful to his father, he had to stay with him all the time and learn the many things he should know. He had to know how to build a camp of *chickees* and how to take care of the family when the weather was bad. Boys were taught that anything they started to do had to be finished.

A father and son would get together and talk about their personal belongings, or they would talk about different methods for catching different species of fish or different sizes. They might also talk about what kind of gig to use to catch a certain fish. Depending on the size or species of fish, they would determine the type of gig or spear to use. They would choose gigs made with two spears on one pole, five or six spears on one pole, or single ones. There was also a special spear for catching turtles.

Fathers would talk about the different sizes and uses for canoes. There were big, medium, and small canoes. All sizes had different purposes. Fathers taught their sons they should use the smaller canoe for hunting and fishing or collecting wood. When taking the family on trips to other camps, they used the biggest canoe. Families had to have at least one to three different-sized canoes, boys were taught. Fathers also taught how to care for the canoes. It was not simply parking a canoe or just climbing in. You had to take care of the canoe every day by keeping it clean. Men and boys cleaned their canoes and enjoyed doing it.

When a boy got older, from sixteen to twenty-two, his uncle started teaching him what he should know. Uncles watched boys to make sure they behaved. An uncle would talk to a boy or punish him if he was naughty. Boys continuously helped their fathers or uncles. They wanted to help because they wanted their folks to be proud of them. They wanted their mothers and sisters to say, "He's a good hunter" or "He's a good boy." Boys were always trying to feed the family and feed themselves, too. They felt good helping the family.

Men who lived in the camps had to find firewood. They always had plenty of firewood for their wives or families to use to cook the food. They did not need anything else except firewood and matches. Another thing to remember is that the husband had to cut at least four big logs to put down a fireplace. Men must always do that so people would recognize the man is taking care of the village for his wife and family.

Miccosukees always ate or used the animals and birds that they hunted. Even feathers were used for different purposes. Women always used wing feathers for a fan when they were building a fire to cook. Feathers were also used when they got dressed for the Snake Dance, or Winter Dance, as it was called. Feathers were used during important types of dancing during the Green Corn Dance. Feathers were used for other things on the Green Corn Dance ground, too. Some of the birds and ducks were what are called "winter birds." When certain types of birds were flying down, that meant winter was here. Some of the birds were not supposed to be eaten. We knew which ones and never killed them. Many buckskins were used to make clothing, shoes, and leggings. The women dyed deerskins dark or light brown. They always had buckskins on hand to make different things.

Men, boys, fathers, sons, friends would get together and go hunting. Fathers told their sons about hunting in low water. Hunting without a canoe was not easy. During times of low water a man walked to get to his destination. Some places he traveled through were mucky. When the water was low, a man had to adapt to changes associated with low water. Since he could not use a canoe to carry his catch to the camp, he would use a *sta-noogee* [pack] to carry it on his back. A man constantly carried one on his back. He would tie it around his shoulders and pack heavy things in it like guns or bows and arrows.

Boys had to learn the importance hunting had for them no matter what life circumstances they faced. Boys did not think about being bored then. They were normal happy children and fully enjoyed their life.

When it was time for picking corn, the family would go to a farm on another island where the corn was grown. Sweet potatoes and pumpkins were also planted on the island, which was three or more miles away from the family camp. The whole family all pitched in to help dig out the sweet potatoes, look for the pumpkins, and pick the corn when it was still green. They would take them home in the canoe for the mother to cook. Everyone in a family worked together to have food on the table, to pound corn and help plant corn. We did those kinds of things all together. Daddy, Mama, children—all of us used to do that. Breathmaker has said to us that we must plant corn yearly because it will be the food and should never die. That's the reason we have the Green Corn Dance. Everything is tied together.

The women always seemed to enjoy pounding corn. At least once a week they pounded the corn to have it ready to make *sofkee*—cornbread—or things like that to eat. It was a lot of work. Sometimes two women each used a heavy pole, big sticks that weighed about thirty or forty pounds. They put the corn in a log that had a big hole in the middle and pounded it with the big sticks. One would pound from one side and the other from the other side. The *kistapee* is a big stick [pestle] that weighs maybe thirty pounds and stands maybe five, six feet tall. The *keyeache* is the big round [wooden] stand on the ground that has a big hole inside. We put corn in there and pounded it. You pound it and pound it, and you can make grits; at the same time you get a lot of cornmeal out of it. In those days we didn't buy corn. We had everything out there. We did it ourselves. Buying stuff, that's come in recently, not in my childhood.

We had all the corn we needed. They roasted the corn; that's one way they did it. They pounded it, too. They ground it and used a different way to make *sofkee*, cornbread, and sometimes we made something like coffee. But with that you don't have to grind it; you just roast it. It looks like burned-up corn, but people boil it like the color of tea. Baskets made of palmetto were used for sorting out the fine-ground and medium-ground corn. They shook the corn in the sifting baskets, and the fine corn went through holes while the bigger pieces of corn stayed in the holding basket. They were important tools that belonged to the women, and they took good care of them. The corn was put in the sun after it was ground. It was put on a cloth on a table to dry it out. The cornmeal was packed away after it was dried so it could be eaten for the next couple of weeks. That was done all the time and kept the women very busy.

Everglades water was used for drinking purposes when it was clean. Water from a type of deep well was used at other times. The rock had to be cracked to make it deep enough. It was good water, and it was also cooler because it was from underground. Mothers always had to have water on the tables for the families to drink or so that people could use it when they needed it.

Mothers would cook different types of foods three times a day. Each mother had a special table where she kept her own pots and pans that belonged to the family. Some food was also dried by putting it in the hot sun on outdoor tables. It was then put in the pots and pans, where it would keep for at least a couple of months. It was boiled to take the salt out before eating it. The women were really good at using the wood to build the fires to cook the food. There was always a big black pot with *sofkee* cooking in it all day long. The corn was pretty good sized when it was ground, and it was put in a big pot to boil in water. It was spooned out to eat and drink.

Mothers made clothes for their families. Miccosukees wore buckskins a long time ago. Women usually worked on the deer hide, and it was a lot of work. After Miccosukees could get different colors of cotton cloth, the women started making colorful shirts for the men and boys. Boys never wore trousers or pants when they were little; they wore a type of shirt that was long enough to cover their legs down to the knees. Many different colors were popular. Every mother and young woman had a sewing machine that they used to make different type of clothes worn during the 1920s and '30s. Sewing was a woman's job, and men usually did not use the sewing machine. A woman often had a little baby swinging in a hammock in the *chickee* while she was sewing. Sometimes the baby had to be swung all the time so it would be sleepy, and they asked a little boy or girl to sit there and swing the baby.

Miccosukee girls learned many things from their mothers. They learned how to prepare food, work on corn, and prepare meats. A girl would learn how to take care of a baby so that when she got older she would be pre-

Fig. 2. Sally Tiger, Buffalo Tiger's mother, preparing a meal with her family at Musa Isle Village. Woman in background is Mickey Tiger, the young girl is Agnes Osceola, and the baby with back to the camera is Annie Tiger. Courtesy of the Seminole / Miccosukee Photographic Archive, Ft. Lauderdale FL.

pared to get married and have her own family. A wife had to be a very stable woman and stay with her husband. The family made sure that a girl understood all these things.

Girls learned their responsibilities from their mother, aunts, or grandmothers. Girls learned how to prepare food and how to take care of the family and home. Before there were refrigerators, girls learned how to dry, smoke, and preserve food such as fish, meat, pumpkin, and potatoes. Girls were taught to share food in the clan camp. A girl learned how to prepare the hide for clothing and to dye it. She learned to stitch or sew by hand and to make the native dress for herself and her family. A girl must learn about her clan and to be proud of it. Girls should have friends in other clans, and they should do things together. Girls could learn all the things boys learn. Girls must learn to make medicine. Girls could ask several women to tell them their experiences of growing up.

In my life, often my people didn't have many material things. We used buckskin or any type of skins we could find. Ladies used to do buckskins, but after that they got cloth material and they started sewing and putting things together. Today they have beautiful clothes, but years ago it was not that way. They were just learning how to use sewing machines, and they cut out materials, different colors. All Indians always seemed to like colorful clothes.

I remember seeing my grandmother and my folks, particularly old ones, that kept their sewing machines, the old-fashioned type of sewing machines. They used to make a lot of noise when you cranked them around and around. You knew your mother was making something when you could hear that. My grandmother used to have one. All old folks had them. They were small; they had no wood around them. No [wooden] frame, nothing like that except the metal. The sewing machines were small, but women used cloth and thread to put things together. It's better than nothing. Many years ago they used a type of fishbone and the tendons of animals, particularly deer. But sewing machines did better work and did things faster.

My mother had a sewing machine when I was born. My grandmother, I'm sure she had done the other type of old-fashioned sewing—not by machine, by hand. But I didn't have any colorful clothing like we wear today. Ours was just different colors put together; we wore it like a little skirt. We didn't have to worry about having too many clothes. If you were lucky, you had maybe three shirts and three skirts, and they had to be washed often. We had to take care of our own clothes, and you had to take a bath almost all the time, particularly us boys. We lived around the water, and our mom would make us wash all the time and sometimes make us wash our own clothes. Then we washed our dishes after eating; out in the Glades water you could do that. That was part of our job, to take care of our dishes and take care of our clothes. Sometimes your mother would wash it for you, but more likely you had to do it.

Everything had to be done. If you were old enough, you had to help your daddy and mama. You were part of the family; you all helped each other. You didn't expect that your mama's going to do it or your daddy's going to do it. You were glad to help, and that is what little boys learned.

Women would dress neatly. They wore many strands of colorful glass beads around their necks. Their hair would be made up by wrapping it around a cardboard shaped like a big hat and pinned down to their hair roots. Sometimes they covered the hairpiece with beautiful beadwork. There were some mothers or sisters who did not fix themselves up like that. They dressed in skirts or dresses made of colorful handmade designs using plain cotton material. The designs were smaller in size in comparison to designs made presently. Mothers, sisters, or women handmade these dresses, capes, beaded jewelry, necklaces, and hair decorations.

Little girls wore dresses, and they were similar to little boys' shirts. Their dresses were a little longer in length but just below the knee. They wore a couple of strands of beads around their neck. Sometimes their haircut resembled a little boy's haircut.

The little boys wore shirts that resembled a little dress. The shirt was a little shorter than a girl's dress. They wore a scarf around their neck. Some wore beads under their clothing. A little girl's dress was buttoned in the back; a little boy's was buttoned in the front. When a boy was young, his mother or relative would usually take a small amount of [spiritual] medicine and attach it to a string of beads and place it around his neck. This way he could carry his medicine around wherever he went.

Grown men used to wear big hats that resembled a cowboy's hat. That was the style of the time. They also wore a band of beadwork on their hat just above the rim. Men wore big Miccosukee jackets every day and night. The jackets had big colorful designs. On the men it looked good. They wore a big scarf around the neck. The colors of the scarf were usually blue, red, and white, depending on the color they liked. The big kind I'm talking about looked very good. They wore pants and shoes too. A lot of people didn't like to wear shoes at that time. I thought they were attractive the way they wore their clothes. That time I was younger so I saw things I liked; I always remembered those things. That was the way it was for Miccosukees.

2

MY BELIEFS

As part of his informal education, Buffalo Tiger learned about the cosmological origins of his people and how Breathmaker, the giver of all life, brought them into being. This most sacred of spiritual beings to the southeastern Indian peoples provided directions governing every aspect of existence—religious, social, and political. The Indians' major annual religious observance, a busk ritual called the Green Corn Dance, was a celebration of Breathmaker's benevolence and a renewal of their cultural unity.

When the Miccosukee people emerged from the earth, they were divided into matrilineal clans that took their names from various totemic ancestors, each with unique attributes that ensured survival of the group. Miccosukees were taught about the origin of the clans and the important role they played in maintaining social equilibrium. They also retained a clear historical understanding of how their ancestors migrated from the Creek nation in Georgia and Alabama, making their way to north Florida and eventually to the Everglades after three devastating wars with the United States during the nineteenth century. Here Buffalo Tiger, a member of the Bird clan, relates his understanding of the Miccosukee people's cultural history and belief system and tells how they have given direction and guidance to Miccosukees throughout his life; he also expresses concern that a new generation is losing these beliefs.

Traditional Miccosukee people, *Eelaponke*, always had great respect for this land, this earth, and life itself. They believed *Feshahkee-ommehche*—the Breathmaker—created the land and all living things. Miccosukee people cherished the earth they live on. They honored it because they knew without it they would not be alive. Without this earth and its elements—air, water, land—nothing would be here. They recognized the beauty of this earth, that from it would grow food for them to survive. They called it *yaknee*—"this land." They appreciated deeply how the land provided delicious crops like corn, pumpkins, bananas, potatoes, beans, tomatoes, and sugarcane. They appreciated how the water provided drink and many species of fish. The land did not only provide plants; it provided birds and other wildlife.

Traditional Indians held deep feelings about the land in part because their life depended on it. Our ancestors taught us to remember we are part of this earth and we must protect it. We must not destroy or sell it.

Today many Miccosukee people are not following their cultural beliefs about the land. They are not practicing tradition in their day-to-day life. The young people are not taught what earth means to their lives. They need to learn and relate to the meaning and develop strong feelings like their grandfathers and their grandfathers before them. Land is more important than money. Today it seems like Indian people think other things are more important. It seems as if Miccosukees are not too concerned for the land. People need to start being concerned and turn back to their traditional practices. Our grandfathers and their grandfathers loved this earth. Because of their feelings for the land, we live here today.

Breathmaker created earth and all living things and nature, and we are part of it. We all belong to what Breathmaker gave. Breathmaker taught us how to live on and protect the land and how to love nature. He taught us how to understand other people but to maintain our customs and culture. Breathmaker has tested us, what we are going to be, what we are going to believe. He's testing us to use written paper, to see if we can live with it. But we were not doing good. He realized that. Then he gave paper to light-skinned people, and they lived with that well. It belonged to them. It will always be that way. Then he asked us to live with nature: trees, life, and how to get along with it. We live in nature and take care of it. He told others how they must live and what they do well!

[34]

We know Florida as the "pointed land." Years and years ago people were always looking for which way to go because it was not easy for Indian people to find food and the right place to live for their people. So the wise people were sitting around all night figuring which way to go. At that time they saw a beautiful tree standing with its limb pointing south, and that meant something. So the wise people spent time together listening to nature speaking to them, and they realized that this tree was telling us to go south. So they sent at least three fellows to check it out; they did, and they found that the "pointed land" was a beautiful place to live, so that's when they started moving down this way. So we know that's how we got here years ago. After Breathmaker had put us on earth, those things happened. We were looking for life to be better for us, so we found a place to go. But don't forget, not all of us moved down here. We lived in north Florida around Tallahassee and were always coming down hunting and moving around. We know this land well. Miccosukees always called it *yugnee-fuskee*—*yugnee* is land and *fuskee* is south, "south land"—but before that it was "pointed land." Breathmaker told us it was here for us to live on, to tend and care for.

We believed that at one time this land was underwater, but then the water drained toward the south. Big animals came down with a big man to where the land was soft. The animals could not go any farther. Different parts of this land are hard rock, coral rock, or soft rock, and in some places the rock is above ground. The east and west coasts are sandy all of the way down. In the central part the land is soft, with rich black or gray muck. There are beautiful rivers up in the north part of the land. There also is a freshwater lake known as Lake Okeechobee.

We know the plants and trees, both north and south. We know the animals and birds. We know which fish live in fresh water and which live in salt water. We had no boundaries on this land, no fences. We were always free. All wildlife and human life could freely wander. Since Breathmaker put this land for us to live on and care for, money cannot buy the land. We are not supposed to buy or sell even a cup of muck. Many of our people have fought and died for us to keep our land.

When they came down here, they found there were a lot of things people could eat. There were five different types of fish in the Glades' fresh water. There were three different types of *yokche*, or freshwater turtles. They found things that come out of the ground that we could eat, too, like a kind of potato and *coontie*. There were plenty of cabbage palms. We could find seven different types of wild fruits that we could eat that grew either in the sand or out in the Glades at different times of the year. Those are the kinds of things they spotted in *yugnee-fuskee*. People wanted to come down because they realized this was the place they should live because there were lots of fruits and things to eat.

Even then, they were going back to Tallahassee, back and forth. They would live down here and hunt and then go back to Tallahassee. They had to make a move, to come down to really live here, because the troops chased them down [in the wars of the 1830s]. The elderly folks always talk about the [aboriginal] Indian people who were here before that. We called them *ouwayachee*—something that lived in the past. Our people did not expect to see them, but they were here. They went away or died. We must have killed them or they moved away from us, so they are not here now. They established so many things like little mucky places or islands out in the Glades. They used to live in different places like that and built the ground up to live on it. We took it from them. That is the way the story is told and what we believe happened.

The Others

We made a big move away from the Creek nation years ago, and we spoke *Eelapone*. Our people lived in Alabama and Georgia; particularly Creek people lived there. There were not too many lakes or fish around there. I was told the reason we never liked the Creeks too much is because they told the United States they spoke for all Indians in the South. The United States believed that we knew nothing about it, but the deal was already made and they came down and tried to take us away. A lot of times the Creeks needed help fighting against the United States troops, and the Miccosukees wouldn't help them because they thought Creeks caused the problems. But we did help them in the last war we had between Jacksonville and Tallahassee [1835–42], and we forced the troops back home for a long time, but they returned to fight us again.

We used to have big villages in north Florida, but they were destroyed and the people separated and since then they have lived in small villages. When Miccosukees finally came out of hiding, there were soldiers camped in the region that now is called Immokalee. The government and Miccosukees decided it was time for peace, so an agreement was made to end the killing of whites and Indians. There was also an agreement to set aside a piece of land in a big area of cypress swamp for the Indians [1842]. Miccosukees really believed that they were making peace with the U.S. government. The killing continued here and there, but only one time involved soldiers. Some Indians got in trouble when they got drunk, killed some white people, and destroyed some of their homes. Those bad Indians were killed, and some of their families were killed, too. After that, soldiers came but did not bother Indians anymore. Indians and other white people did not bother each other either, except for a few troublemakers.

Miccosukee families with children then began to feel good about things. Miccosukees love their families, and those who still had children cared. Some of the people who did not have families really did not care anymore. They were the ones who wanted to stir up trouble, and they were killed for that.

There were a few incidents of white people who killed Indian people because of egret feathers. Egret feathers were worth a lot of money. Some Indian people took feathers to sell, thinking they would get paid for them. Instead, bad white people killed the Indians and took their feathers. The same thing happened with skins, like otter skins and other different things Indians had to trade with white people. There were some very bad people around the Glades. There also were some good people who had successful businesses of trading clothing, cloth, and other things with Indians. They welcomed the Indians and let them stay on the porch or yard at their stores or houses. Indian families went to the store, traded, and then went back into the Glades.

Many people from Europe came here to trade with Indians long ago. Indians traded feathers and buckskins to get the cloth and colorful glass beads that the Indian women liked. Trade was friendly at first, but our people remembered there were some Europeans who became enemies because they were taking advantage of the Indians and killing them. It made the Indian people angry, so they killed them. Trade went on for quite some time with the Spanish, British, and French. Our people saw that they were all light-skinned people and called them white men. They recognized people from the different countries. They thought that some of the French and British people were friendly, but they must have been closer to Spanish people from time to time. There were many Spanish people in the Everglades area. It was easy for Miccosukees to learn Spanish, and they used words from that language. English was harder for our people to learn.

Trade continued for a long time, so our people decided that was the way their life was going to be. They could hunt for different hides to sell and did not have to work to earn money. People mostly bought different types of animal skins and feathers that were popular. Our grandfathers, grandmothers, and uncles taught that Miccosukees must learn how to be good hunters because they could always sell skins and feathers. They then could buy the things men needed, like farming tools, axes, knives, and guns, or could buy pots and pans, beads, and materials for the women to use to make clothes. These were new things for our people. They started to wear clothes of materials and no longer wore buckskin clothing.

Our Names

We call ourselves Miccosukee Indians, but that is not our real Indian name. We are *Eelaponke*—and have always called ourselves that. That has always been our name for our people.

We have always called the Seminole Indians *Cheeshaponke* in our language. They are another group of Indian people, not of our group. We used to be with the Seminole Indians years ago, but we broke off from them. We have a different language. We have always lived down south, down in the Tallahassee area, while the *Cheeshaponke* lived in Alabama and Georgia. People started calling them *Simano-li*—Seminole. That is how they got their name and began to call the tribe that. The same is true with Miccosukees. The Spaniards and other people started calling us "Miccosukees," so we began to call ourselves Miccosukees.

We know who we are and what type of language we have.

The Miccosukees live around the Everglades. Sometimes we lived around the Big Cypress area, but we do not call it "Big Cypress." In our language we refer to "where the cypress trees grow" and know the people who live there. We call the people who live around the cypress on the West Coast different nicknames. They call us *Eelaponke*, and so do other Indian people.

Miccosukees always used dugout canoes made out of cypress; Creeks called us people who lived with boats or something like that because they always saw us in canoes. Many people called us fish eaters or fish hunters or something like that. We call our people by names that identify where they live, what they do, or what they eat. Miccosukees are known to always use a canoe in a lot of water and eat fish, while the West Coast people eat some different types of food than we do. They probably have deer and beef more often. Our people also live on turtles, birds, and deer.

It is important for you to know what we call the Everglades. "Everglades" is not in our language, but it is where we have always lived. Some of our people call it *Paheyaoke*—"River of Grass." Sometimes people call it *Ashaweayaoke*—"Where the Cypresses Are." And others call it *Chooyayaoke* —"Where the Pines Are." Pine trees grew on the sandy soil.

The Clans

Eelaponke came out of the earth. Breathmaker created us out of the clay; it happened to be brown muck, so we turned out to be brown persons. He had put us down under the ground, and we lived there for a long time; then it was time for us to come out and we did. We were Breathmaker's people, and we came out years ago because it was time to come out. There were about twelve clans; now there are about seven clans among the Seminole and *Eelaponke*. This has always been important to our people because that is the way Breathmaker planned it to be.

It took Breathmaker to make the animal type of clans, the Bird clan, the Snake clan; they are all living things on this earth, and that is what our clan would be. Our blood does not come from the animals, but these are things we are supposed to remember. The Panther clan was supposed to come out of the earth first, and the Bird clan was supposed to be next, and others were to follow, but it did not happen that way because the Panther clan's heads were too big—when you see a panther animal its head is pretty big—the hole was very small, and they couldn't get out. So they asked the Bird to get out because bird has a little pointy nose and the head is small. So the Birds did come out first and helped the others. The Panthers came out next, and the other clans followed. So Bird clan always has to be close friends with the Panther clan because we helped them to get out. The Panther clan always asked the Bird clan for help. The Panther clan is not the peacemaker. Sometimes they want to see peace, but they cannot make it last long so they always ask Bird clan people to come make peace for everyone. Big City (Frog) clan can make peace also.

Sometimes other clans asked special people like Bird clan and Big City clan to help with problems. They are the ones who tell us what to do and how to do it, but they cannot do it themselves. But the Panther clan and other clans are in charge of spiritual medicine. The Wind clan is a very important clan, too, because when we came out it was dark and there was not much air. The Birds could swing their wings and give a little air, but not much. The Wind clan made the wind blow, and we got air and light. So all of the important people are supposed to work together to make things better for us. And all the other clans are the followers, like the Frog (Big City) clan, so that's why we are in different clans. Breathmaker made us; that is the way it's meant to be.

The Big City clan is an important clan when discussing important decisions that have to be made. So any time that trouble takes place and we had to go to court—we used to have court to punish our people, either death or just punishment—a Big City clan member would be the last person to speak. If he had decided what way it was going to go, that's the way it would go. Many times we did that at the Green Corn Dance and any time we had a major problem; it could happen anywhere, not just at the Corn Dance.

There are not many clans left. Only seven or eight clans still exist in Florida, and these are made up of Seminole and Miccosukee members together. Clans had a very important function at one time. They still do today, but we ignore many things that we are supposed to do and forget how to respect each other. We are not too concerned about it, but we should be. It is a part of our way of life that was given to us by Breathmaker. We should never forget about it and walk away from it. If we do forget about these important things, sooner or later we will find that we are sorry we did.

All Miccosukees belong to their mother's clan, and our clan is very important to us. Clan members share food and other things not only with our own camp but also with other clan camps. Visitors often came to the camps by canoe; family members or other people would come along. They were always asked to sit down at the tables and offered water to wash their face to cool off for a while. We would give them some food, and they would talk, enjoying themselves as they visited for a while. When they were ready to leave, they were given food to eat while they were on their way, wherever they were going. Everyone seemed friendly. Every clan is proud of its role in the Miccosukee community.

When we get married, we have to marry into another clan, not our clan, because we have to protect our blood. That's the way it has always been. That's how Breathmaker made us and told us who we are. Boys are taught that if a girl is in his own clan, even though she is a cousin or second cousin, it means she is his sister and he is her brother. You have to treat her like a sister. The same is true for girls. A girl treats a boy or man who is a cousin like he is her own brother.

Every time you see a village out in the Everglades, it always belongs to a clan and to the grandmother or mother. A village has to be of one family. We are all brothers and sisters in the clan. It is important to know that, and that is why we identify a clan. We always have to know if you fall in love with a girl or woman and you want to marry her, she has to be from another clan or another village.

At one time a girl did not have to fall in love with a man or boy to marry him. A girl's family would select someone who they thought would make a good husband, who would take care of her and help support the family. He had to be a hard worker, plant corn every year, and learn how to hunt well. Parents of both clans must agree to the marriage. The boy will leave his clan camp and live in the girl's clan camp until they have a few children. Then they may leave the camp if they choose and establish a home of their own.

We should recognize that the different clans have their own camps or their own villages. Each clan has responsibilities. When there were problems or any sickness, people used to get together and talk about it and decide what should be the best thing for us. Each clan must have a place to speak.

Miccosukees did not set up the clans the way they are or make the law. Breathmaker told us that we are to live this type of life and to set things up this way. Some things had to be changed recently. When changes are to be made, Miccosukee people from different clans would meet and discuss many things. They would then decide if they should try another way to do things. Sickness is an example. There was too much sickness here on this earth in the early days. People from different clans met and decided to gather it all together and had a bird fly as high as it could to take it up in the sky.

Clans have to be respected. They used to be, and we need to do it now because we are not too concerned about our clan or the clan of others. We have to be careful. We don't have to hate anyone. We just have to love ourselves more and respect ourselves more. Respect the other Miccosukee people more. We should also respect each village, each clan. When we get together, we should discuss the types of problems we have. If we don't, we are going to be losing some of the things we are talking about.

Spiritual Healing

Some clans are responsible for taking care of spiritual medicine, and other clans can do body medicine too. There are some clans that cannot do spiritual medicine. Today we call the people in clans who do spiritual medicine, medicine men. We need to learn more about this, which clans have the right to spiritual medicine and their members can be medicine men and which clans cannot. Spiritual people could be Big City clan, could be Wind clan or Panther clan; most of the time it is the Panther clan.

But not everybody can be a spiritual person or leader. It depends on how the man was born, what happened when he was born. Our people decided something happened when he was born, something odd or something different. They know that when this baby, this boy, is grown up, he is going to be different, and we want to ensure that he learns much more because he will be important.

Some spiritual people learned faster than others. They can make medicine quick; they can protect the other people and help them keep spirits close by, or make medicine to make them go away. A good spiritual medicine man studies medicine about four years. Medicine men learn in nature; they have to be with nature to see things to understand. They have to keep practicing through their life, as long as they can. They go back and try to see what Breathmaker told us to do.

This type of spiritual medicine existed for a long, long time before the white man ever put his foot on this earth and on this land. It's been with us a long time, and our people have looked after that. Our spiritual medicine is so precious to us, and it has given us strength. In a way it is like when Christians go to church and pray. It is almost like that. Our Breathmaker does look after us, and we all know that. Spiritual medicines can be used for health medicine or body medicine, too. It works both ways. There are lots of other people who can make medicine for our bodies or sickness and things like that, but they cannot be spiritual medicine men. The two are different, and we have to understand that, too.

Miccosukees used alcohol, or *keehoome*, for medicine. Many people would take a drink, not to get drunk, but used it as medicine because they believed that using alcohol helped them to learn more. You can forget certain things in making Indian medicine if you stop learning. They used *keehoome* to make them feel good so they could listen and learn, but they also knew that too much could destroy you.

You have to learn how to make medicine for the people when you are young. Some of the older people would come to the camps and sing for the young people to teach them. They would tell them what they were singing and how to make medicine. Some of the young people quickly learned how to make medicine. The older people explained the types of sickness and what they did to treat them. The type of medicine used depended on the type of sickness a person had. Different types of roots, leaves, or bark off of trees are used for medicine, and the sick person had to know what to gather for the man or woman who was going to make medicine for them. They were also told what present would be appropriate to give to the person for making medicine. Sometimes a medicine doctor wanted a chicken, or cloth in such colors as black, white, yellow, red, or blue. People sometimes might give a little pig.

There are times when you can see a man or woman making medicine and you can hear them singing. When Miccosukees are making medicine, they always have to sit facing the east. After he or she takes care of the singing, they blow into the water or into a type of little bucket. If water is used, it could be boiled with the medicine in it. The sick person might drink it or take a bath in it. The medicine doctor might blow in a little bucket and then add water, and then the sick person would drink or bathe in it. Sometimes they just would burn it and smell it. There are different ways to do medicine, and it works for us. Sickness that Miccosukees used to get was natural types of illnesses, and the medicine doctors were very good at taking care of it.

When a sick person was asked to do certain things, he or she had to do as they were told. They might be told not to take a nap that day even if they were sleepy. There might be certain foods not to eat or certain things not to do for four days, and then the person would be back to normal again. Sometimes it might take four months to be cured. Many people have said that it takes either four days or four months.

If the medicine needed for an illness was not already in the camp, people sometimes had to go very far to get it. Someone might have to travel in the middle of the night, or night and day, to get the medicine or find the person who could make it. Not everybody can make medicine, and our people know the certain people who can do it. Miccosukees learned to respect the learning of the people who do medicine. Many people have been sick and got better. It was important for parents to know what type of sickness a child might have when they got sick and to do something about it right away. Sometimes they just got better by themselves.

Death and Change

A change we made a few years back was how the dead are buried. Our people used to bury the dead underground. When we die we have to go back to the earth because that's where we came from. Our bodies want to go back to the land wherever we are. But the spirit has to go away; it is harmful if it stays around too long. Medicine has to be made to make the spirit go away. Many times they come back, but most of the time they stay away. When we bury a person, it's with the head toward west and the spirit moves away toward the west. Not to a particular place like California, but in the general direction. We still practice this, so we are different from other people on that. The problem was that the spirit stayed in the body if it was buried underground too quickly. The spirit would be closed underground. People decided that we should put bodies on top of the ground.

Miccosukees put away their dead by traditional custom or by non-Indian way. Whichever way the deceased person is taken care of, white or Indian, they are laid with their head pointing in the direction of west. Miccosukees have always believed the spirits go west, into the darkness. That is the reason why babies, children, and adults are not to place their heads facing west. Miccosukees can lie down with their head pointing in any other direction: north, south, or east. The sun goes down toward the west. Some elements relating to the west also present risks to Miccosukees. It is custom that when a baby, child, or adult is sleeping during late afternoon around sunset to awaken them from their sleep. That means to disturb their sleep for only a few seconds. Miccosukees believe they must not sleep through sundown because their spirit might leave them. And to prevent this from happening, they awaken each other to disturb their sleep for a moment's time. This practice ensures their safety. Miccosukees know their spirit will eventually go. It might happen today or tomorrow. They know their spirit will leave them at any time. It can happen when sleeping and when their head is pointed to the west. It is especially true when a baby sleeps through sunset, or else the baby can get sick when it sleeps during sundown.

Miccosukees believe all directions are related to colors. The west in color is black—*looche*, we call it. But we should always start in the east. East is yellow—*lakne*—where the sun rises and light. Every direction has a name. The north has a name too, but the color is red—*keteshche*. South is white—*hatke*—it is like the beginning of life. All those four colors we use all the time. When people make medicine they use that, and we live in it. That's how we believe, and we cannot forget because Breathmaker has taught us. Inside those colors are lots of things that only people studying Indian spiritual medicine know. Let me give a little example: the east looks like anything you find in food; most of the time when it is ripe it is yellow. When it gets a little older, it is a little darker, in some places red. West is when something is not good and you cannot eat it; if meat is black, it is no good. White is just the beginning of everything. That is the way we see it, and the spiritual people see so much.

Miccosukees learn about other circumstances that relate to pointing westward. They learn that west is unsafe for the living. West is for the dead, not the living. Many, many years ago the United States government captured Miccosukees by the multitudes and resettled them in Oklahoma. Traditional people used to call that place *Okeehome*—it means "Bitter City." "Oklahoma" comes from the Miccosukee language. People knew that Oklahoma was located in the west and reasoned it was an unsafe place. Miccosukee people believed they should never go westward because only a dead person's spirit goes westward. Even so, some Miccosukees accepted relocating in the west and settling in Oklahoma; some were forced to go. Miccosukees who remained in the South knew this was a move they should never have taken. Their lives would be unsafe because they knew at death their spirit leaves and goes to the west. The spirits also go west during sunset.

Miccosukee people knew that anything coming from the west would be bad or unclean. They believed that if it came from the direction north, south, or east, it will be good and they would be pleased with it. Miccosukees were taught and still are that if a Miccosukee travels in the direction west, they must be at peace with themselves before they go. Someone will caution them not to go because they will not bring anything good back with them.

Another change that the people decided was needed was about our houses. They decided the fresh air is good for us and we should live outdoors. We used to live inside in log houses, and it was not healthy. People got sickly, so they decided that we should live outdoors and have no sides on our homes. The fresh air then could go through our homes and where we were sleeping and living. That is why we always lived under the *chickees* with no walls around us.

Those two things—not putting the body under the ground and living inside of houses—are changing back to the way we used to live. Some traditional people prefer to be put away by not being put underground. They want to go the traditional Indian way. It is done many times, but most often the bodies of Miccosukees are underground today. We also have started living inside of houses again.

Those changes were made without permission from the people in the right clans telling us we could make changes. It was decided the simple and easiest way. That is also the way white men do those things. We seem to be moving in that direction in the way we live and the way we do things. That is why it is important to recognize that the clans must continue to be consulted in making decisions.

The Green Corn Dance

There is a place where our people get together to celebrate Green Corn Dance. If you plant the corn at the right time, there will be a time to eat green corn, and that is why you celebrate the Green Corn Dance. It is very important. Our Breathmaker decided to give us another day if we first managed to hold ourselves together and do things he told us to do. It is simple. You grow your corn and take care of it. A man and his wife are supposed to save the corn each year for planting next year. Our folks told us so many times we must save a bunch of corn when we get old enough. When the corn is dried up, you are able to save the seed. Put it in a jar or something so it is kept fresh until you are ready to plant. Our people have done this over the years, and we should continue to do that. We must plan to do those things so we will have green corn. Don't forget to save them when they get old and dried up. Save that for next year to plant again.

We do a lot of things in the Green Corn Dance and on the grounds that keep our ways and our culture together. People used to have courts at that time. So many times people would get married during that time. People would have fun playing ball. They would take medicines, drink medicines. There were all kinds of different things that would take place there. Young boys, young men got new names, their man's name. They always got their new name there. There is no place else where you could get your new man's name except at Green Corn Dance.

Each man and woman had their responsibilities. At the Green Corn Dance ground all of the camps have to be respected by all of the different clans. I respect you and that is what I would like for you to do for me each time you go to Corn Dance, each time you stand there right in front of the Big Courthouse; we call it the Big *Chickee*. The many camps belong to different clans when you go to Corn Dance. Corn Dance is held on one big island or hammock, but the camps are separate. They are set in a semicircle facing the Big *Chickee*.

Miccosukee adults get scratched for a good reason when they go to the Green Corn Dance. A lot of men get scratched a lot on their chest, back, arms, and legs. It is said that is done because their blood gets too heavy. You carry around heavy blood and must let your old blood go. New blood then comes in, and it is not as heavy. This is still done at the Corn Dance.

Young people knew that once a year they had to go to Corn Dance and they had to learn how to dance and sing. They could learn how to make the different types of medicine made for people when they got sick if they chose to. Miccosukee young men get new names. Really it is not a new name; it is an old name because names live on. They will keep the name until they die, and then someone else will be given that name. Many different dances take place all night or all day. Boys only get men's names when they have danced the men's dance all day and all night.

Who is in charge of the Corn Dance ground? That always has to be the Bird clan. Whoever was the medicine man at a particular time used to discuss things, but the Bird clan was in charge of the Corn Dance grounds. That is the way it was understood, and this has been going on for a long time. It is simple how the Bird clan arranged to get that. That is the way it is, and people respect it.

Medicine men are spiritual people who are qualified and have the right to be in charge and take over spiritual medicine. The spirits of medicine that the medicine people have for us have come from a long way. It came through many, many years. It came through different men, but they have to care for us. They have to care for us because they understand its strength. All of their life they lived around it. Also, they understood that each village was their responsibility.

If you went today to the Green Corn Dance and medicine people have medicines, you would probably have a chance to look at them. In the next hundred years maybe you are not here, but another young man will look at it again. It is supposed to go on and on and on until the earth is destroyed. That is a time we should really behave and think about ourselves and think, "I must be a special person to be here. We must be special people to live on this land. Even though white men wanted to destroy us, we are here and we are going to be here, and we love what we are because our Breathmaker is looking at us."

Breathmaker gave us all the things we do, and food, and strength, and our spiritual medicine. They are good things. We should respect the type of things he did for us and gave to us. We are here. We have the strength to be here and alive. We want to live on until such a time he will be speaking to us again. Look for his guidance, particularly on the Corn Dance grounds. Most Miccosukee people know what to do and what it means. There are some who don't know too much about the meaning of the Green Corn Dance anymore, but a lot do. Sometimes we overlook some things that are the most important. We need to talk about it and try to learn more about why this happened or that happened. It's going to happen again and will happen again maybe in the next hundred or maybe in the next five hundred years.

Our Stories

We do have many types of stories about different things, but mostly about animals or the birds or different things. We learn it from our grandfathers, our grandmothers, our aunts. Maybe the Seminole people or the Creeks can tell stories almost same as we do. We don't have too many people to tell stories now. I remember when I was younger we heard them every night, every night, every night. It was important for us to listen. Those things we listened to and learned. Again, you can train the child with that: training and learning experience are all together in the way we see [things].

The one story I always liked was: Two Miccosukee young men, good friends, agree to go hunt. Maybe two, three days they wanted to go away from the village. They were going to walk, so they got their things they're going to use, like a little food to eat, a little blanket, little things, spears and things like that. They carry them off, and they walk all day, away from the camp. So they found a hammock, way out there. The hammock was too big so they find a little place they can spend the night on the ground. The two friends, one of them said, "Well, you go ahead and fix the little camp where we're going to spend the night, and I'm going to look for firewood so we can build fire and fix the food to eat before we go to sleep."

The friend started fixing the ground up so they could lie down and sleep on the ground, and the other young man was chopping firewood. While he was doing that, he just chopped a big tree. There were gallons of water in it, fresh water in that tree. Sometimes the tree has water in it, so I guess this time it must have happened. But it's a story. And a big fish was in it, not bass, but a bream. Bream, nice and fat so both can eat.

So he found it and was all excited. He says, "Look what I found for our supper." His friend says, "Where'd you get that?" He says, "I got it out of wood. When I chop wood, water come out and fish jump right out. So we got supper here now; we're going to eat it." His friend says, "No, you got him out of the wood, out of the water out of the wood?" He says, "Yes." "Okay, we're not going to eat fish because fish should be in the lake or in water, not in the tree. You don't find any fish like that, so if you do find them we shouldn't have to eat it. Just throw it away." "No, no, we're going to eat him." So they made an agreement. [The first says,] "I'm going to go ahead and cook and eat it." His friend says, "I'm not going to eat it." It's a deal they made.

His friend [the first young man] turned [into] a snake before morning. So he says, "Go tell my people. Go tell my sisters and brothers and all people in my clan. Let them come see me before I make a move. Also, after that you go find me a lake. I'll be moving into lake while you go to get my people so they can see me." So he did that. He got up, and he was a big, big black snake sitting there. But he was not mean. He was still talking then. So the young man looked for a lake and found one. So he told him he found a lake for him. Snake said, "I'm going to go to lake from here, and you go tell my people, my clan, particularly my aunts and my mother and my grandmother. Let them come see me; otherwise they think you did something wrong to me, and I don't want that to happen." Snake said he would give a signal. "When you come to lake, stomp the ground four times and holler four times, and I will let big bubbles come out four times. That means I'm going to come up."

The boy went back to his people to tell them. "My friend ate a fish, and he got to be a snake. He told me to come get you so he can talk to you." Right away everybody started accusing him, saying, "You did something wrong to him; you killed him." He says, "No, I didn't. He told me to get you so he can talk to you. I want you to go with me, and I'll show you where he would be." They didn't want to go, but some of them said, "Let's go find out. Let's see if he's telling the truth." So he took his people out to the lake. It was a long way to walk, but they finally got there. They can see a big snake had been crawling around; they can tell that.

They didn't see it, so the boy did what Snake told him. He stomped the ground four times and hollered four times. Snake let four bubbles come up, so then he knows he's going to come out. He did come out—a big, big black snake. His tongue stuck out like a snake when he gets angry. He came toward his people; his mother and grandmother and one of his aunts couldn't take it. She got weak and fell, almost falls in the water, but she did not. Snake came up and lay on her lap. He told them, "I'm the one that did it. My friend told me not to eat fish, but I did it because I thought I could do it. I shouldn't do it, but I did. I did it wrong. Despite what you were teaching me all the time, all the years, I did it wrong. Now I am a snake because I have eaten fish."

Those are the kinds of things adults were telling us. When you have friends, you're going to have to be careful. You could do something; you can hurt your friend, or you can get in trouble. Or you'll find something out of place. Don't eat it. You shouldn't be eating when you find it, whatever it is, in an odd place. So we always have to remember that.

Our Way

Years ago young people never thought that their elders or themselves were dumb. They generally thought their grandfathers and fathers were smart people. If you ask why, the answer is, because of them we are here today. They faced hard times. They endured and survived war. The white man murdered Miccosukee Indians and treated them wrongfully. Yet through all of this they stood up for their belief that this land is part of us. They wanted to live in their homeland and die there.

Miccosukee people all shared this belief and strong feeling for the land. They were smart to have thought that way. They did not learn their philosophy from non-Indians—white men or Spanish. Miccosukees simply believed in their beliefs. We believe in *Feshahkee-ommehche*. White men and other races believe in God or Jesus. *Feshahkee-ommehche* taught us our beliefs.

It was crucial that our grandfathers protected the land themselves and survived. This is why we must never think things like my mother or father is dumb. They are not dumb. If we find ourselves thinking that, we are the ones who are dumb. It is important to remember our grandfathers were very smart and that's why we are still able to exist in our native land.

We were taught by our grandfathers, fathers, mothers, and uncles that we should not get angry when we know something is not true. We should be able to be at peace with ourselves and to make matters better for ourselves. We Miccosukees should always know ourselves. We should place our feet solidly on the ground and not let anyone say that we are worthless beings. If you as a Miccosukee are able to identify with your ancestry, you will know yourself. If you know your identity and practice it, no one will ever be able to condemn you as worthless.

Another tradition taught to Miccosukees was that they should never think that they could defeat the people living around them. The people living around them were the white people. The white population outnumbered them, and they reasoned that they would have to learn to live together as neighbors. They did not have to be enemies. They simply needed to know themselves, their past and present history, and the events that led them to a moderate adaptation of non-Indian lifestyles.

Miccosukee children were taught that they are not supposed to make fun of older people. Older people are to be respected at all times. Whether a man or woman, they are the ones to always ask questions of because they have lived through many years of experience and learned from the past. Older people should always be treated with respect by all. They should be allowed to eat first and be consulted about decision making. There are many things to know about courtesy to your family.

Miccosukees were told long ago about marijuana and other drugs people talk about today. They grow like little weeds. This is the way it was told by the older people: The wind was blowing from the east by the bay in late afternoon. There was a beautiful voice that sounded like singing. The people looked around but never found anybody, and the noise stopped. That happened again on another day. This time people wanted to make sure they found whoever had that beautiful voice, a lovely-sounding woman's voice. They thought they would see a woman and started looking around to find out where she was. They got closer and closer and saw a plant standing by the beach. When the wind blew, the noise came from the plant. It was the leaves making a noise exactly like a woman with a nice voice singing. Then they realized what it was. They were told it would be used like a type of drug at a later date, and it would be so strong that everybody would drift into using it because the smell was so powerful. Everybody would want to smell it and would get closer and closer. We were told many times to remember that it would be very powerful and to be careful with that plant.

People used to be in more control because they knew Breathmaker's law. It's the only law we know. It is simple. We didn't make that law. Breathmaker thought that was the type of law we must use, and we lived with it.

White men can make a law today, and it can change tomorrow. Our laws are not supposed to be that way. We are supposed to stick with whatever laws we were given. That's it. We have to learn to show respect and to behave because we were taught that. It looks like we have no laws if we don't learn that. It looks like we have nothing and that only the white man has laws. That is not true. We do have a law, but it is not exactly the same thing as white man's law. We didn't know and we didn't care about the other law. Today many people think the same way. White man's law has existed, but it's not clear to us because we have never learned the law.

If you know and believe in your own law, or what we call Breathmaker's law, things are okay. Sometimes there is confusion that there is no law. When people mix up our law and white man's law, we become confused about which way to go and what is right. It is not the way we have been taught. It is fine if you are going to learn white man's law and your own law and try to understand both. It can be done, but you have to understand it clearly. A lot of times we do not know our own law and do not know all of white man's law, but we think we do. We need to learn more about our own laws. Then we can move into another area like learning about white man's law.

3

LEARNING THE WHITE MAN'S WAYS

Florida Indians have interacted with non-Indians on a limited basis since the last quarter of the nineteenth century, when they carried on an intensive trade in bird plumes, otter pelts, and alligator hides with white storekeepers. Indian families would make camp for several days at Fort Lauderdale, Miami, or other towns while trading, then return to their Everglades villages. Around the time of World War I commercial tourist attractions featuring "Indian villages" opened in Miami and other Florida cities, providing Indians with an opportunity to spend protracted periods in the white milieu in a relatively safe environment. When the Tamiami Trail opened in 1928, it brought more Miccosukees into the tourism business when they opened their own showplaces along the federal highway. Buffalo Tiger's family was frequently in residence at one of the urban attractions for at least part of the year. The young Indian learned English through interaction with outsiders rather than formal schooling. He also understood how to deal with non-Indians and live in their culture; he married a white woman and moved into Miami to raise a family. These experiences prepared Buffalo Tiger to become a spokesman for the Miccosukees when their independent existence was threatened by the federal government in the 1950s. In this chapter Buffalo Tiger recalls the preparation for his role as a mediator between the Miccosukee people and the outside world.

Many Miccosukees today do not know how the Tamiami Trail was built. Some helped build the road or saw how hard the construction people worked to build it. Indian people knew no name for the Tamiami Trail when it first was started, but there were important changes for Indian families after the road was completed. Non-Indian people considered building the road "progress," but our people did not think about it that way. They thought it was not a good idea and did not care about so-called progress at that time. The Dade County portion of the road grading was completed by 1918, but it was a long time before the rest of the road was finished. A small canal had been dug, and a narrow road was built on the side of it. The road was rocky and bumpy, but it was good enough for the Model T Fords to run back and forth from Miami on it. At first the road just went up to an area known as Pinecrest, a hammock with pine trees that was a few miles from where the big curve at Forty-Mile Bend is now. Sometimes the water came up too high and ran over the road. Many snakes and fish came up on the road and got stuck there.

The Florida State Road Department took over construction of the Tamiami Trail in 1926. Miccosukee men who helped to build the road did not work on it all the way through. The road goes east and west and curves like you see it now at Forty-Mile Bend. Miccosukees never worked too far from this [east] side of Forty-Mile Bend. There was a camp that had a store and a few temporary houses where non-Indian and some Indian construction workers lived while the road was being built. The non-Indian workers had Model T Fords, but the Indian people did not have cars. They still used dugout canoes for transportation.

Miccosukees had small jobs like cutting cypress, but they worked hard and got paid very little, about fifty cents a day. They were not paid in real money but instead were paid in coin. It was not United States silver coin. It was light like aluminum, and each coin was worth twenty-five or fifty cents. The workers could only use the coins they were paid with to buy groceries in the store at the camp. A lot of the Indians who lived there had a problem with drinking alcoholic drinks that Miccosukees call *keehoome*, which is liquor or whiskey. There were bootleggers around, and it was easy for the Miccosukees to get too much *keehoome*.

The Tamiami Trail was completed from Miami to Tampa and opened on April 25, 1928. After that, Miccosukee people at first still lived just as they always had, using canoes to get around, planting corn on the islands, and eating a lot of pumpkins and fish. There was plenty to eat.

My people did not move around that much when the highway was completed. We did come in here [Miami] and pick up groceries and go back. I remember my dad once coming in; he couldn't decide whether to use a canoe to come in and pick up some groceries and go back, or to walk. I was with him, and he said, "We're going to walk." We were way out there about thirty miles outside of town. I wanted to come in anyhow, so we got all ready and began to walk. Someone came along in an old broken-down Ford pickup and stopped and picked us up, and we went into one of the stores in Miami on the Trail and he bought some groceries. After you buy that much groceries, people will be happy to take you back. My dad knew that, so we went back the same day. We didn't mind taking a walk even though we were a little afraid because we don't trust people that much. We were kind of selfish, I guess, in a way, but that's what we felt at that time, that other people were not always good friends, although some were.

Another time my dad wanted to come to town in a canoe, and I was supposed to come with him. We did, and it took us a couple of days, maybe a day and a half, to get where we wanted to go. We went in on the rim canal along the Trail all the way down to the Miami Canal, and we stopped around Flagler Street. There was an old bridge across, and underneath was an old frame house sitting there, and they were friendly to our people. It had a big porch, and any time Indians came in they could stay there a couple of days and buy whatever they need and put them in the canoe and take them back. It was the only place at that time, but they were friendly.

We stayed on the porch, and in the morning we got up and took care of washing our faces and everything, and he wanted to know if I wanted to go with him. I said no. There was a little horse pulling a wagon around delivering ice. I was supposed to stay on the porch, and I did.

The people who lived in the house were friendly and wanted to know if I was hungry, but I couldn't speak English. You know what those people gave to me? Hamburger with mustard and onions, and iced tea. The food just tasted horrible! I couldn't eat it, and I couldn't drink the tea. That was the first time people had given me that type of food, and I thought, "Do people eat onions and mustard that smells that bad?" But I was thirsty and would drink Coca-Cola, but not tea. I have no idea how old I was then, but it was some time ago. When my dad got back, we spent the night there, then got back in the canoe and we headed back. It took us a couple of days to get back where we started.

On that canal were all kinds of bushy places. There are buildings now, but we hardly had any buildings then. There was mostly trees and ponds. It looked nice but kind of wild. I enjoyed pretty much seeing that. The water was moving, and you really had to paddle hard to make the canoe go the way you wanted. It was a dugout canoe; sometimes we poled, but sometimes it was too deep to pole and you had to paddle. That's what we did, and I'm sure other families did, too.

Tamiami Trail Camps

Some Miccosukee families began living in camps along Tamiami Trail after the road was completed. They opened gift shops to sell souvenirs in front of their camps on the highway. They sold beadwork, skirts, jackets, and dolls. The families opened up their villages to the public, charging maybe 10 or 15 cents admission so that they could make extra money. Other Miccosukee people started saying they should not live there. They thought it was harmful for Miccosukees because they would adopt the non-Indian lifestyle.

Several families continued to live along the Trail anyway, and others built new camps. John Osceola, John Poole, William McKinley Osceola, Charlie Billie, and Willie Jim opened villages in the 1930s. These tourist businesses were all operated by Indians, and some did pretty well. Some of the camps that were started back then still exist today.

John Osceola and his family built a camp at Monroe Station. John Osceola was of the Big City clan. His wife was the Bird clan. They had a big family of five daughters and three sons. The daughters married and moved away, but some still live in the area. John and his wife lived there until they died. Today John Osceola's son, George, and his family still live in the camp. George and his family maintain it the way it was meant to be, as a camp and village. They opened another village, but people did not stay there too long, so they closed it down.

John Poole built a camp in one place but left it and moved to another lo-

Fig. 3. Miccosukee children at Musa Isle Village, ca. 1933. Buffalo Tiger is at right in the top row. Courtesy of the Seminole/Miccosukee Photographic Archive, Ft. Lauderdale FL.

cation. John Poole, his mother, sister, and other people who lived there built a village and gift shop at the new location. John Poole and his mother were Bird clan, and they both lived in that village until they died. John Poole's wife was from the Otter clan. Their daughter married Bobby Billie, from the Bird clan. Bobby Billie's wife passed away, but Bobby kept the village. He has remarried, to a woman from the Otter clan. John Poole's village still exists today. Bobby Billie lives there, and the village is kept the way it was originally.

Charlie Billie and his wife, an older woman, started a village at a location between John Poole's camp and the camp of Willie Jim's father. The village was located where there used to be a gas station. It was a big village at that time. Charlie was a traditional Indian man from the Panther, or Wildcat, clan. His wife was from the Bird clan. Both he and his wife lived there until they died. Their son, Chesnut Billie, was a smart and likable kind of guy, even though he was not popular with everyone. Chesnut Billie maintained the camp after his parents died and enjoyed his life there.

Charlie Billie's daughters and their husbands went on to establish another village on Palm Hammock where another camp had been for a while. Today Panther and Bird clans are running the camp.

In 1935 or 1936 William McKinley Osceola established a very nice camp in the same location where it is today, at Thirty-Mile Bend. He and his wife built the camp, and they had a good business of selling crafts in the village. William McKinley was of the Big City, or Frog, clan. His wife, Alice, was of the Bird clan. They had a big family with many daughters and sons. William McKinley and his wife lived there until they passed away. The camp is still there and should be kept the way the father and mother took care of it during their time. Virginia Poole and her husband live there today, and the Bird clan is still keeping the village.

In the late 1930s and throughout the 1940s Frank Willie had a camp where the Miccosukee Tribe's Indian Village is now. Back then his camp was a small place with hardly any land at all. It was built on a little island and had a gift shop. Frank Willie was Bird clan.

Jim Tommie's camp was located near where Mary Osceola's camp is today. Jimmy was of the Panther, or Wildcat, clan. His wife was of the Bird clan. They left this camp, and it perished in time.

Jimmy Tiger established a camp near Jimmy Tommie's camp. Jimmy and his wife and his family lived there. Jimmy Tiger is Bird clan. His wife was of the Taakoshaale clan. After she passed away, Jimmy moved into Frank Willie's camp. Frank Willie turned over his camp to Jimmy Tiger, as they were both from the Bird clan. Jimmy fixed up the camp, and Frank Willie helped him build the village. Today this village is owned and operated by the Miccosukee Tribe.

The Miccosukee village and other camps started this way. It is important to know how those camps were started and who started them. While this happened in the Glades, all the families lived a traditional life, hunting, fishing, and life with nature. The people who built the camps long ago made something out of them, and they should be remembered. No one told them what to do, not even the government. They did it themselves and took care of themselves well. The clans of the families who lived in the camps also should be remembered. The Indian people who adapted so well to business have made history, and it is important to acknowledge their accomplishments. They might not have made much money, but they had a lifestyle that they enjoyed.

The Commercial Villages

There were other types of Indian villages in the city of Miami. They were commercial exhibition villages. Henry Coppinger and his family opened a village on Northwest 20th Avenue and the Miami River in 1914. It was called Coppinger's Tropical Gardens. An Indian camp had been located on the land for many years before Mr. Coppinger bought it. Coppinger's was a nice village because they had beautiful palms and other tropical trees. Many people came from the city on a boat to see the plants and trees. Miccosukee families went about their daily activities so that tourists could see how Indian families lived. Miccosukee people did not have a chance to sell the crafts that they made to the public. They were only allowed to sell what they could to the owner of the gift shop.

Musa Isle Indian Village was another village in Miami. This site had just started out as a juice stand, Musa Isle Grove, on the Miami River at Northwest 16th Street and 25th Avenue. The owner asked my uncle Willie Willie to open a large camp on his property in 1917.

Willie Willie liked to go in to Miami to socialize with white people, and they liked him too. Willie Willie got the idea that Indian people could make some money if they set up their own place in the city. He was the kind of person who spent all of the money he made. His father, my grandfather Charlie Willie, didn't trust him; he considered him the "bad boy." The family put all of their money together, about five thousand dollars, to build the village. Charlie Willie asked William McKinley Osceola to watch over their business and see that the money was handled properly. Willie Willie was Bird clan. Charlie Willie and William McKinley both were of the Big City clan.

John Campbell bought the land where Musa Isle was located in 1922. Bert Lasher took over the village from Willie Willie about that time. Musa Isle was open for many years. The Tiger Tiger family, William McKinley Osceola's family, Sam Willie's family, and other families lived there. Other families lived there before them. Then Bert Lasher took over. He drank too much and wasn't too good at running the village anyhow. I can't remember that, but I was told that.

Willie Willie moved and established another village in Hialeah in 1924 or 1925. Some of the people he knew asked him to open a village, which he did. I guess they loaned him money. Many Indian people went there and

Fig. 4. Buffalo Tiger, age 18, painting Indian crafts at Musa Isle Village, 1938. Courtesy of the Seminole/Miccosukee Photographic Archive, Ft. Lauderdale FL.

helped build the *chickees* and everything that needed to be done. We went to Hialeah and stayed there. It was near Palm Avenue and close to the railroad track. The Hialeah Racetrack was nearby. Many Indian families lived there, and they thought that the people were friendly. White people who were going to the racetrack used to stop at the village to see Willie Willie and the Miccosukee families who lived there. I can't remember too well, but there were people friendly with Willie Willie. I always thought it was because he was friends with Al Capone. Al Capone [and others] came in big, black cars, about two or three cars, in the village to see Willie Willie. I think they were on the way to the racetrack right next door. That's what they were doing.

The Big Hurricane

In 1926 a hurricane came through and destroyed the village. We weren't there. We didn't stay there all the time. We were just coming in maybe three months, four months, and we would go back. The attitude my family had was to go in there maybe a couple of months and come home. Get those dollars and come home with materials and food. We used hundred-pound bags for so many things, you know, and then kept them and used the food. We went back, and a hurricane came along.

We happened to be in the Everglades at this particular time. About three or four families got together and wanted to go out in the Glades, looking for alligator skin or anything they could kill for skin. About three families moved around in canoes.

We were coming in this way [to Miami] from out there about this time of day [late afternoon], and it started raining and getting windy. Our people said the weather's bad. So this particular time, I just thought it would rain and the rain was going to be finished. But our people were so particular about it; they wanted to go somewhere on a bigger hammock with hard rock. They wanted to find higher ground.

We got out, cleaned [the boat] out, and then were fixing dinner, and it started raining hard. The wind started blowing hard, so they put canvas on top of the poles so we could sleep inside. We had mosquito nets, but the wind kept blowing harder and harder and harder. Pretty soon it started picking up the candles we had, blowing them away. This time they had to let us know it was a hurricane coming, so the old men had to get up and move away from here. [The adults said,] "We have to find a place for you." So my parents did, and by this time it must have been about three o'clock in the morning.

The wind was blowing so hard, we could hardly walk, and it blew everything around. There was an old big tree standing there, but the limbs were all beat up, blown away. Then what they did, they put their canvas around it and they tied it up somehow. They tied it down real good. Then they put us in there, a bunch of kids, maybe four or five, my family. By this time it was so bad you couldn't walk. All the trees were blowing away.

Many times you saw the snakes crawling all over, trying to get away from the water. Meantime the canoes were rolling around in the water, and our guys were trying to keep the boats from blowing away. By this time water was all around us already. Good thing they found a high spot, higher ground; otherwise we would have been in the water. It was so cold and so windy. We were all wet, babies and everybody.

We survived because us kids moved together, and we used all kinds of blankets to keep ourselves warm. Even though our faces were cold, our bodies were warm.

This real, real bad hurricane wind started blowing this way, then started moving around this way, moved around this way. Wind started blowing this way, hurricane coming in from the southeast, winds blowing from the southeast, then it blew from the northeast, then started blowing around from the west, then blowing from the southwest. So that's how they saw it and knew it was going to be finished. A big dark bird with its tail like two sharp points sticking out came flying by, flying low. That bird was not seen here at that particular time of the year. It was windy, but we knew it was going to be finished. Our folks were happy it was going to be finished.

It was gone now. Then we were so cold, I remember that. I was so hungry. That time of day could have been between five o'clock and six o'clock [A.M.]. Then we ate what was left. I can't remember what we had, but whatever it was we ate. Might not have been good, but it was good for our stomachs. Got something in our stomach, and we felt like going to sleep. You know where we would sleep? A wet blanket—we didn't care. We slept on a wet blanket, and we slept good because we were tired.

The next day was beautiful sunshine, and we got up to look and we didn't see nothing. It was like an ocean. Our canoe was still there, and all the trees were blown away; if not, they were just lying in the water. My folks said, We're going to have to go home. I guess this particular time they realized there's nothing at our home either. But we guessed we were going to go home like when we left, *chickee* and everything. But when we got home, it was not like that. Everything was under water. Everything was blown down. But we didn't mind because as long as we had each other, we felt good.

The experience we had in that hurricane I will never forget, even though I was a little guy. What did we try to do? We got so cold. We had a little brother I was talking about, Bobby Tiger; he was a little guy. The [children] wanted to hold him because he was warm. So we just passed around the babies and kept ourselves warm. We got through it, and we went home, and half the place was broken down. *Chickees* and all of it were under water. It was not easy to find food. There was just too much water. Let's say you saw turtles. You could get them, but when turtles saw you at a distance, they just went under water. You just couldn't see them anymore. Same goes with the alligators. Everything was so hard to get because there was too much water. We didn't go hunting because we didn't go that way [north] looking for deer. We just stayed around our area and tried to find whatever we could. We managed.

Everybody lost their camps. *Chickees* particularly were blown down and blown away. At that particular time my grandfather—I believe he had passed away maybe not even a year. My grandmother was with us, and Willie Willie was in that village in Hialeah. Some of the people stayed with him, and the whole village had blown down. When we went back to look at the village, everything was gone, and we did not see our uncle; this was early. He went to the Hollywood reservation, and the other families did not want to go to that reservation, so they came back to the Glades.

Different Worlds

Everybody called that [Hollywood] reservation Big City, but it had nothing to do with the clan name. That's where my uncle Willie Willie went. He had a little gift shop and a little store. My mother, my aunts, and the families said, "Let's don't go see him." I believe a year later it was decided we ought to go see him. We took the bus to town, and we took the bus to Davie, and we walked from Davie to the reservation. It was hot; I remember that walk. I was a little boy, too. When we got there, Willie Willie had a little gift shop and had little Coke drinks in cans and things like that, but in this little broken-down house. He was living there, and he had no place for other people to sleep. He managed to get a place for us for a few days. He had one of those Model T Fords. He brought us back on a truck; that is how we got home. He got sick and died there.

We went to Musa Isle when I was still little. When Bert Lasher had it, we were there for a while. Then we went to Hialeah. Then we came back to Musa Isle. I remember in the 1930s we were at Musa Isle during winter when tourists were here; then we came back in summertime to a little village out here.

Our parents wouldn't let us go to school. If you had a pen in your hand, if I did that, I got a whipping. They didn't want us to use a pen because it was the beginning of reading and writing. If we went to school, learned English, we would start losing our ideas, liking the other people's life, not our culture. So they wanted us to stay in Miccosukee life; they didn't want us to get into learning anything in English. I got a whipping over that a few times.

We used to play with some of the non-Indian boys. We loved to play baseball. We loved to play football. Any game they played, we liked to play.

But we didn't do that so openly. We did that when we can, when our folks didn't catch us. If they saw us doing that, we got a whipping. But we do that. I think my cousins and other friends liked to play, so they were doing that, too. Knowing if we got caught we're going to get a whipping.

You know, I was one of the bad boys. I'm pretty good in other ways, but when I want to do something, I am going to do it!

As far as learning English, that's how we picked up English. Some of the people, boys and girls, wanted us to speak English, so they helped us learn it. It's funny—we never taught them to speak our language, but they wanted to always give us English-speaking lesson. They loved it.

As far as school, around 1934 or 1935, somebody had the bright idea they were going to put an Indian school at 27th Avenue by the bridge near Musa Isle. There used to be a big hammock there, and they put up frame houses, small houses, and it looked like an Indian camp. It was supposed to be a school for us. We lived in Musa Isle, and we could go to school there. But our parents and people told us that the school was going to be open and if anyone came from the school, don't go back to the school, don't go with anybody. I just didn't go to school. We were afraid to do that anyhow, so we never went to school there. The little building sat there for a long time. I don't know what happened; maybe a hurricane destroyed it.

Willie Willie tried to get me going to school. He talked pretty strongly to my mother about why he felt that way, and my mother listened to him. I happened to be there listening. They were saying on account of land you have to live in the future because everybody buys property. Land is not going to be open for our people to live any way they wanted like they had been doing. Plus all game and food was not going to be there, so you have to work. You have to know how to speak English. You have to learn how to write English. And they were going to put a telephone and electric wires everywhere. So there was no place for us to go hide. If somebody found you doing something wrong like taking animal skin and selling it to people, they would call the law on you. Law is going to get harder. Let this youngster go to school. He can learn how to defend you.

So my mother said, "No, he stays." She got real angry and started crying; then I was afraid, too, because I was just ten.

And our folks hated him, hated him so bad. When he got sick, my aunts and my mama didn't go see him. My oldest aunt went to see him to stand by when he died. They just hated him so much because they couldn't forget what he was saying. He didn't do it; he was just advising them that they should. That's the way it used to be. It was so hard for us to talk about going to school—you couldn't do that.

My Name

You have to have a baby name. I have never heard the names alike in Miccosukee, always different. They usually come from many ways. A lot of times people used different types of medicine when a baby was born. It could be medicine, could be anything that happened at that particular time to name a baby. But most of the time it comes from being some part of the medicine. So that's how we get our names. Even the girls get it and boys get it. The girls usually die with their baby name. A boy, when he gets old enough, gets a man's name. Most of the time when you grow older, you forget the baby name. But I remember mine, and I think some of the people remember their baby names, but other people don't know.

The second name or grown-up name comes from a man's name. You have to be around maybe fifteen or sixteen years old. Just when you can do without food for twenty-four hours, or at least a couple days and one night. You have to do without food, without sleep. Then about three in the morning you get a name. Everybody knows you do that at the Green Corn Dance. The name comes from someone, a man that had been passed away for maybe three years. Later you can take that name and give it to your son if you want to. But I think it goes with the clan, too. A lot of times a man is a bad man; I don't think people want to use that name.

Boys won't have a name until parents find a name. If they think their son's a good boy, they want a good name. Then they fix it with the clan, and they bring him in. Parents don't name you; the medicine people, the traditional council are the ones that give you a name. Your mom and dad suggest a name to them, and they take it and study it a bit to make sure the name is okay for this young man. Then they call him. It's kind of a big deal, particularly with us.

I got a name, maybe three or four boys were with me, and we lined up and they called you. You come in, and your daddy's with you. You come in, a big fire is burning, you're standing there, and the council is just sitting. I'm not talking about the elected council; I don't mean that—the traditional council. They talk to you, who you are, who is your daddy, who is your uncle, and what clan you are in and that kind of questions. You should tell them you want this name. They said, "We're going to give it to you," and they tell what you've got to do after they give it to you. You're not going to eat, you're not going to sleep until daylight; when the sun comes out, then you can eat and you can go to sleep. And you would do it. You had to agree to that. Then the medicine people, at least one man, got up and said this young man is going to get the name and who that name came from and when that person passed away, and he is qualified to take that name, and we're going to name you; and they do that.

My name is Heenehatche. He was someone who died, and my dad and mama wanted me to take that name, so we had to go to the yearly Green Corn Dance to give me the name. So when you are finished and you are coming home, you've got a man's name.

Then I got older and started hanging around the commercial village. I loved to play ball and liked to play with other kids. Even though my dad and mom and our folks didn't want us to do so, we still played. We started learning how to play games like baseball and football that school kids, white boys, liked to play at that particular time.

My baby name was Mostaki and man's name Heenehatche, but people around the village couldn't say that. They were going to give me a nickname—not Indians, but the white people, particularly the older guys. So they were watching us play games. They said this young man runs like a buffalo. Let's give him a name, Buffalo. They did not say Tiger; they said give him the name Buffalo. Then it would become Buffalo Tiger. My father's name was Tiger. It's the beginning of like a nickname. So people started calling me Buffalo Tiger, and next thing I knew, I am Buffalo.

Going to the Outside

I started working in the Miami area villages in the 1930s, but not to have a big job or a good-paying job, just something for us to do for dimes or quarters, which was okay then. Some of my people could speak no English at that particular time because we never had gone to school. Our folks wouldn't let us go to school, and they themselves had not gone to school, so no one spoke English hardly. So when they had to go buy groceries, we were old enough to ride in the car, if they had it. People took them to the grocery store and let them buy groceries. We helped them out, particularly the older folks—aunts, and grandfathers and our mothers; we used to help them in that way. In working with our people, what we are supposed to do, we learned that from our parents. Every time some Miccosukee people came from out in the Glades and wanted some help, we never said no, and helped as much as we could.

Like if they wanted to go to the doctor, we helped them in English as much as we could. We were not speaking too well either, but we did what we could, particularly myself. I used to know many doctors here in Miami and worked with many old doctors, but they passed away and we found another doctor like Dr. Reintz. Dr. Reintz used to have an office on 36th Street and 17th Avenue in Miami; he had two sons who had gone to school to become doctors. He was a nice fellow, and we spent a lot of time with him even though we didn't have a contract like today. We never got any help from Indian Health Service then. We used to go see the doctors, and we paid them a little money, and we would buy our medicine. We did a lot of that, and I know many people were trying to help Indian people at that time. They helped us to learn more English, too. The doctors were real nice—let us in offices and explained many things; that's how I learned lots about sickness. So I did help a lot.

We were old enough to play and work. We got a little older, and we started drinking beer, but not very bad. Then we started making friends with non-Indian people and got to know them better. I had a cousin Mike who wanted to go to school; his dad was William McKinley Osceola. Maybe he said to go to school so he could help Indian people someday. Maybe he could be the spokesman one day. So he went to school, and he did well. He did play football and finished school. He had fun and made lots of friends.

When I had grown up, during the war I used to work building airplanes. We made planes for the navy at a plant on 36th Street where Eastern Airlines was located. There were two other Miccosukees working there at the same time, my cousins Homer Osceola and Mike Osceola. The foreman was a nice fellow. He would walk by and say, "Buffalo Tiger, Buffalo Tiger—I really don't like your name. We're going to have to give you a better name." I said, I don't care. He said, "Well, we're going to call you William." Okay, that's all right; names mean nothing to me. That's where

William comes from, the foreman at the factory. Then you put it together, William Buffalo Tiger. That's how I got each paycheck. I didn't ask for it, I got it!

I did not serve in the army during the war. Most of my people opposed the draft at first. I registered for the draft and wanted to volunteer, but my mother didn't want me to go. I belonged to the McAllister Volunteers, a home defense force sponsored by the McAllister Post of the VFW. We wore regular brown uniforms like the army.

Marriage and Family

When I was old enough—maybe I was not old enough—I did marry the first time a young woman. Her first name was Ann. How I met this young woman: I used to work at Musa Isle Indian Village, and her parents worked there. So we got to know each other for a long time. We got a marriage license; I didn't know too much about it, but we had to get a blood test and we got married like other people in city life.

I still helped my people when they came in, particularly some of my aunts. My aunt lived out in the Everglades, and her husband was a real old guy, and they came in to see us. We were living in a house but not a fancy house, just a place to sleep. They came to see us, and they finally got to like the woman I married. She was a young white woman, and I was a young Miccosukee man. They got to like us, and they invited her out to their camp in the Everglades. They had a little village—their own homes on islands.

One day we went back with them and spent some time, and they liked this young woman because she did so many things for them that they never had people do for them. Like little cuts, bruises, sores, whatever—we always used a different type of material to bandage all that; they used different colored material. She taught us not to do that but use white materials that were clean so no germs could get in. We never thought about it that way. That kind of thing she did and people liked her for. And not only that, when a baby was born she helped them to change the diapers. Years back, I guess we all know, we didn't have these throw-away diapers like we have today. We had to wash them and hang them and let them dry. Those kinds of things she started teaching them. She helped them to deliver a baby, but sometimes a Miccosukee man didn't want her to deliver a baby. But my brother Tommy had a wife and a couple of children at that time, and another one coming, so he asked my wife to help and she did. She took care of them good, and the husband told her what to do, and the baby was born okay. Those were the kinds of things people liked, and they accepted her pretty well.

We did so many good things for the people. I didn't think we were doing good things, but I can look back and we did because we tried to help out all we could. After the people accepted me to be spokesman, that's when she got deeper into tribal affairs. After people saw how we were, they thought maybe marrying a white woman was not too bad and I was okay, so they thought maybe I could be helpful being spokesman. It took them a long time to decide that I am the one, just about one year I had to wait. They let me know that's the way it was going to be. I had to listen to them, had to always be honest with them and stick with my people, particularly the traditional beliefs. It is pretty strong, and I had to learn; and they helped me learn that.

But my wife, Ann, could not be Indian yet because she was still white. All the things she did they accepted that pretty much, but she would not be Indian, would always be white. Because, they told me (the medicine men themselves), you have a white woman who is good and everything. [They told my wife,] "We're going to give you a few years, and if you can prove yourself and still want to come in with us, we can make you brown. We can change you to brown." They didn't mean skin changes to brown; spirit is brown. They said that happened years ago; some of our people used to do that: when a man and a woman were so good to help Indians and died for it, they would make their spirits brown so they would be one of us. They would do something called "making medicine" for them. As far as your body, it never changes; but your mind is like one of us. They were afraid if she stayed the way she was, she would change her mind and walk away from us, and they didn't want that to happen. They wanted her to die in our life, like I would die among my people; then she would be the same way. But she never did that, so if she ever died she would be gone the other way. They taught me that's the way it would happen; if she wants to stick with you, we will do that, and we don't have to be afraid of her. Years ago people did not trust the white man, so that's what they were looking at. She wanted to do that, knowing she would have to go through something to get there, and I knew that too. She spoke pretty well in Miccosukee. She was good learning the language quick. I believe everybody seemed to like her, but it did not make my life change. I was still married to a white woman, and even though they liked everything, my wife was still white.

Those days I almost forgot about because I was just trying to help my people and take care of my family—it was hard. That particular time I didn't have any job I could work making much money. But I was pretty handy making crafts, so we made a lot and she was really good helping me, painting; we were both making and painting. We used to go all over the state selling and making a little money from that. That's how we lived; we didn't have a job; she didn't have and I didn't have a job for ourselves. And the work we did for our people we didn't get paid, but we had enough to live on.

My wife was still young, and she had to go back and finish high school in evenings at Lindsey Hopkins [vocational school]. She did and was smart enough to get a scholarship to Miami University. We had our minds made up when she went back; we wanted her to be a lawyer so she can help our people. She thought she could help me a lot if she was a lawyer. So that's what we planned to do, but it did not work out; everything seemed to change. She went through college at Miami University, and she studied different languages. She spoke very good French, and I believe that is what she is teaching today. I heard she is still teaching in the state of Florida. We never hear from each other anymore.

So to end up, we had to get a divorce, but we had two boys. One we called Steve Tiger and the younger one is Lee Tiger. We lived in Hialeah at that particular time, so they were going to school in Hialeah. The time Lee and Steve were growing up they had a hard time. Their mother left them; at least I was there. They did have fun. They played with the Miccosukee boys; they could fish and do what Miccosukee boys do. After they grew up, they had ideas, their own minds. I didn't agree with them. I thought they were better off growing up with what they had to be. I told them they had to leave. They were gone for two years. They went to New York and California and returned home. They had different feelings, and we got along fine. They wanted to work with Miccosukees and help set up the village. They helped develop marketing and tourism for the tribe and the Arts Festival and the Music Festival. They were good at doing that.

Steve has a lot of talent in art and music. He's an artist, so he realizes where he's from and he seems to see the colorful culture of his people through his music and paintings. Steve works for the Miccosukee Tribe. Now Lee Tiger has his own marketing and promotion business. Lee has one daughter and two sons; two children are grown. Steve has five sons; some are grown.

Later I married another woman, and she was not Indian either. Before that I was trying to marry Indian girls, but I was turned down two times. I didn't feel that good, so I started to go another way. Then I married a farmer's daughter. Her name was Phoebe. She was real nice, a hardworking girl; she helped me, and we picked up my life again. We were married by license and [attorney] Morton Silver . . . he married us. We were still working on crafts, still trying to help my people, still working with them. We were more in politics at this time, in pretty deep. I decided to get my people some kind of medical help. I'm sure she always remembered that; sitting at the table, I told her that's what I wanted to get. We contacted so many people.

At this time we lived in Hialeah, and I was working for the tribe, trying to get something going. Everything seemed to be not going well for them. We had no help from the government; they had no reservation. They were not recognized by U.S. government. So we wanted to help them get those things so they at least would have some protection, some rights, and some help from the U.S. government that they needed. So that's what I was working on. It was very, very hard, and finally we got those things.

After we got recognition, the Miccosukee Tribe could work with the U.S. government; then my wife worked hard with me, and we established things out here for Miccosukees. She was helping me at the restaurant and all the places I tried to get going. Because those days my people, very few could speak English . . . so it was kind of tough, but people had faith in me and stayed with me and worked with me, and I had some help from non-Indian people. We had Bureau of Indian Affairs' employees to help, too, because they were with us at that time. Anyhow, it got to be too much for me. Every day I would go home and drink some beer, and it got to be too much for my wife, my ex-wife; she didn't want me to be drinking. For some reason I had the hardest time giving up my drinking habit. So she left me for that; took the children and went back home to where her folks live. Later we got divorced. I continuously supported my family, my children, to finish school and to have medicine and doctor bills; however I could help them, I was there to help them. I helped them to become grown up, but I got divorced. That time it was painful because I loved my family so much, but I had to realize they were already gone and not much I could do. But I stayed home because she left the house to me; she wanted to get paid later. So I did that.

We had one girl and two boys. The first one is William B. Tiger Jr.; he is an engineer in Detroit. Sally finally finished college in Tallahassee. She is married to an engineer, a non-Indian. The younger one, David, used to come down and see me often. I can't remember if he finished college or not, but he finally married and lives in Tallahassee and bought some property there. They are successful, more than me!

When I got married again to a white girl, it was rough. It was not easy, and I knew that when I got married. My brother Jimmy used to be pretty hard on me. He was older than I am, and he didn't think that I had good sense to do that. People told me some places my wives cannot go, like Green Corn Dance ground. They could go around the camp or village, but not go inside the dance or take part in the activity. They could not do that. After I got married, I could not do that either because I was married to a white-skinned person. We could watch, we could do things like eat with them and all that, but some places I could not go. In particular my wife could not.

I told you, all the medicine people said white women had to have medicine like Indian. We had to be treated like it happened years ago during the wartime. Their spirits are still white and Indian spirits are brown, so they had to make medicine, strong medicine, and they had to stay put for so many days, and spirits had to change to be like ours, so they can be sure she stays with me forever until she dies or I die. She's not going to quit by walking away or divorce; that's what they were afraid of when you married outside people. Some of them were real good to my wives, and they did everything for them and all that, but they always had a feeling they were not part of us. They're different. That's what they always thought.

One of the elders talked to me, I said earlier. They said that in marriages like that, they can be married and live anywhere they want to live, but not in Indian country. If they did, all right, but if you bring your wife into Indian country, it seems to be that added a little problem. Then, second, if you are a leader or medicine man, you have an important position you are holding for the tribe, and that seems to be a problem. That's what the medicine men told me.

I waited a long time to remarry. What made me do that was a lady I know well. She happens to be half-blood herself, partly Creek or Seminole. Her name is Betty Mae Jumper. She told me, "Mr. Tiger, for some reason you had a hard time keeping a wife." I said, "Yes." [She said,] "You just don't have to get married next time because she might leave you again, because for some reason you're not keeping your wife. Next time, you just go ahead and have your girlfriends, but don't marry." I said, "You think that's the way it is for me?" She said, "You can get married, but they're going to go again. You're going to get real hurt again. You know that can happen to you, and it can happen again, too. Just think about what I say to you," and I always remember that. I remember what she said to me. That made sense because of what happened to me.

A Tribal Spokesman

In years back Miccosukee people usually selected someone as their spokesman. But for some reason they said those people were not doing a good job. Sam Jones and all the medicine people got together and held meetings and meetings and meetings. They had meetings in Hialeah, out here, all over. They did not like what they saw, and so they finally came to my brother Jimmy Tiger. He was a hunter and had a broken-down car. He had a village, and he did a little more than me. I was an unknown guy. I was living in town. I was young and doing anything I wanted to during this time when they were looking for someone, a certain man. So they came to my brother and asked him to be spokesman for the leaders. We call the leaders medicine people. This particular time my brother said no, he did not think he would be interested in being picked. He thought I could do a better job. Of course, I could speak better English, and I had been around people in the city. I knew the white man's ways pretty much. So he suggested, "Why don't you select my brother? He is more qualified than I am." So they said they would listen.

So back in around 1952 they came to me; Sam Jones and all the medicine people, they were here too. They all came to me and said, "Your brother told us that we need to talk to you," and I said, "Okay."

"We are interested in a man like you to speak for us, talking to the government; and we want you to talk when we say we are ready for you."

I did not say no. I said, "All right."

And that was all they said: "We will see you again; we will talk to you again." I waited and waited and waited and forgot about it.

One year later they came back, the same group, and said, "We are ready. Now you are going to speak for us." They said, "We've been watching you—how you work, how you do things. You accomplish what you start off to do. You are a good one. We want you to speak for us. But you're still young; you do not know about everything. But we are going to be telling you what to say and what to do; and when you get older and have more experience, we do not need to tell you. You just go ahead and do what you learned from us. You pick it up from there." And I said, "Okay."

So they let me speak for them, and I did not speak good English, but I knew a little. During the war I had gone to Lindsey Hopkins [vocational school] for a few months to learn to read and write and got about six grades of school.

Miccosukees had problems that developed in the 1950s because they did not deal with the United States, state, or county governments. Miccosu-

Fig. 5. Buffalo Tiger explaining issues to tribal elders. Woman in front row is Ann Tiger; next to her are medicine men Ingraham Billie and Sam Jones. Courtesy of the Historical Museum of Southern Florida, Miami.

kees lived as Indians as they always had. They did not see changes that had started taking place because they lived in the Glades and were busy hunting every day. They just lived for game or fish. Some Indian people started to notice that wardens from the Fish and Game Commission were visiting Indian camps and making trouble with the families. The wardens wanted to know what they were cooking and eating. They tried to keep us from eating garfish, mudfish, or whatever fish we usually eat. The people did not like that and knew they had to do something about it. They brought the situation to the attention of the Seminole agent in Hollywood, but nothing was done to stop the visits from the game wardens.

The medicine men and other leaders realized that their people had no protection, so the same or different kinds of problems could happen again and again. They knew that there were no state or county laws passed at that time to protect them and they had to do something to protect themselves. A lot of changes would have to be made, and it was going to take a lot of work to fight what was standing in the way of living their traditional lifestyle.

I kept learning; I'm interested in that. And I realized I needed to learn a little more English, too. So I made up my mind I would go back to school, and I did ask permission from the head medicine man. I was working with him, and he told me it was all right for me to go because I'm a grown man and they don't have to worry about me.

I made up my mind who I was. I went back to school at night, adult education at a big school, Lindsey Hopkins, in downtown Miami. It was an old school, and anybody wanting to learn any type of education can go there. You can go at night; you can go in day. I used to go at night. I wanted to learn English and maybe a little math. I was worried about handling all kinds of different numbers, like lots of money. I learned a little of both. To me, that helps me improve English. I realized I needed it because I was dealing with so many people. I had to deal with the people at Washington level and in different tribes, different types of people, and the state of Florida. I dealt with the governor and the people who work with him, and county business and all that. They have all kinds of different laws and different meanings, and everything is so different from what we learned. I was trying to learn that.

I worked with a young lawyer, a Jewish young man [Morton Silver]. He was young, I was young; we both worked together. We both were not get-

Fig. 6. Buffalo Tiger meeting with Commissioner Glenn Emmons, 1955. Next to Emmons is his assistant Morrill Tozier, then Morton Silver and an associate, Leo Alpert. Courtesy of the Historical Museum of Southern Florida, Miami.

ting paid. Nobody told us how we were going to get paid. But someday he would get paid, but I did not. I never thought I would get money out of this because I was spokesman for our people and I love my people; they considered me to be spokesman, and that made me feel so good. So it's the pay for that.

As my first job, I was asked to speak to government people in Tallahassee for the Indian people. I was still pretty green. So we got together with our people—I'd say at least fifteen Miccosukees—and Bob Mitchell of the Seminole Indian Association. He happened to be living in Orlando at that time and had a place for us to stay. He said come up and let's do something about it. So we came up, and he arranged for us to meet the citizens of Orlando and people in government, the mayor and all. They were having elections at that time so we got in at the right time, and everybody came to us—

newspapers, the radio, and all that. So anyhow, they wanted us to call Tallahassee and talk to the governor, so we called him and the governor was not there, but the governor's aide happened to be there. It was nice; he said the wardens are just going to have to stop doing that to you people. Later we found everything was straightened out, and they never bothered us anymore for that.

Meantime, we were trying to get my people to work with the U.S. government, but they didn't want it for many, many years. So I quit trying to work with the Bureau of Indian Affairs. They saw in Hollywood for many years a superintendent who sat there and never did anything good; they knew that and thought all the bureau was like that—and they were right. But I finally convinced the people to go ahead and try to work with the Bureau of Indian Affairs.

4

THE STRUGGLE FOR RECOGNITION

The decade immediately following World War II was a difficult time for American Indian tribes as they struggled to retain their lands and political sovereignty. Congress, dominated by fiscal conservatives, seized the opportunity to reduce the size of government and balance the federal budget by eliminating agencies such as the Bureau of Indian Affairs. What ensued has become known as the "termination era" of American Indian policy. The goal was to terminate services to Indian peoples on the reservations as well as to sever the nation-to-nation relationship that had historically existed between the federal government and the tribes. The Florida Seminoles were one of the tribes singled out for termination, but they escaped that fate because of the support of Florida's congressional delegation and other state leaders. In 1957 the Seminoles organized a federally recognized tribal government, allowing them to retain reservations and promote tribal business enterprises. The culturally conservative Miccosukees declined to join the Seminole Tribe and began to agitate for their own land and tribal government. When federal authorities balked, Buffalo Tiger and other Indian leaders visited Cuba and secured recognition from Fidel Castro's regime. Embarrassed by contact between a Native American community and a Communist dictator during the Cold War, Washington relented and allowed the Miccosukees to organize their own government. In this chapter Buffalo Tiger recounts the problems that Miccosukees confronted in gaining recognition as a separate Florida tribe and how they created a constitution tailored to their needs and values.

The Shadow of the Seminoles

There is a difference between *Eelaponke* and *Cheeshaponke* in language, life-style, and government. In the 1950s we realized that we lived down here being *Eelaponke*, in the water, hunting and fishing and riding in canoes. We have always known the people living up near Lake Okeechobee were riding horses and had cattle. We call them *Cheeshaponke*, and we call ourselves *Ee-laponke*, as we have already talked about.

Some of the Indians, *Eelaponke* and *Cheeshaponke* both, wanted money for the land that had been taken from us way back in the last century. They wanted to make the government pay us for that. Some of the Miccosukees and some of the Seminoles' members, both *Eelaponke* and *Cheeshaponke*, had established themselves living on the Hollywood reservation and the Brighton reservation in the Okeechobee area. They wanted to go ahead and file a suit against the United States because some white lawyers suggested it. They wanted to sue the United States government for many millions of dollars. It was not really for the Indians. It was for the lawyers themselves. Some of the Indian fellows listened to them and wanted to go ahead and sue the government.

This was before the Seminole and Miccosukee tribes were organized and had a constitution, and first we had to be recognized by the U.S. government like we are today. Lawyers should not have filed a suit against the U.S. government on behalf of both tribes for payment of the money to the Seminole tribe or Seminole Indians—but they did. This was a time when our people, *Eelaponke* and *Cheeshaponke*, seemed to be looking at each other suspiciously because some of our Miccosukee people did not want to [file suit] and some did. Some of the Creeks, *Cheeshaponke*, did not want that suit either, but some of them did. The lawyers went ahead and filed a suit against the government for the Seminoles even though the government did not recognize both tribes. The suit was set up under the way they ran the cattle business on Big Cypress, Hollywood, and Brighton reservations. These reservations had what were called "cattle trustees" at that time. They went under that title and filed the suit against the United States.

That is when the battle started. All Miccosukees did not want to be a part of the suit, particularly our older people, and they opposed it. Most of the Seminoles wanted to go ahead with the suit. It is important to understand that not all of them wanted to, especially the older people, because they knew that is not what we are supposed to do. The younger people went ahead and did that. Our people and some of the Creek people opposed it too. There was not much they could do because they could not speak good English and did not have lawyers to fight for them. We had lawyers down here, O. B. White was one, but he was not opposing that suit. We had different lawyers speaking for the tribes. John O. Jackson was the lawyer the Seminoles used for filing the suit against the United States for money payment.

That is what made us look at each other, and we kind of hated each other at that time in the 1950s up until about the 1960s. Miccosukees did not want to go along with anything the Seminoles did; we did not want anything from them, and we just kind of hated each other. That is the way it has been all along because people have always been thinking differently, particularly the Creek people, who were always doing different things that the Miccosukees did not agree with. That is why there was a big split many years ago [in Alabama and Georgia], and that is what happened again in the 1950s.

In 1957 the Seminole Tribe got all of their reservations and was controlling them. Before the tribe was organized, there was some money that had been collected from leases on reservation land for oil, cattle, and farming rights. The government had been holding the money until the tribes were organized. The Seminoles asked the Miccosukees to meet with them. I was working for the Miccosukee elders, the medicine people, and they went to see the Seminoles. Maybe twenty or twenty-five tribal people went with me to the meeting. The Seminoles wanted to know if Miccosukees wanted to share the money they had because they were getting ready to spend it. I told them that the people I worked with like Ingraham Billie and the rest of the older people agreed they did not want to accept anything from them and told me to tell the Seminoles they could have it. They were happy to hear that, and we never got any of the money from them.

Another time, when the Miccosukees met with the Seminoles again, they said they were going to share the cattle they had. The cattle came from some place in Oklahoma. The tribes were supposed to take so many of the cattle and put them on the reservation and start a cattle business. Again, I was told to tell the Seminoles that the Miccosukees were not interested in the cattle, did not know how to take care of them, and did not have a reservation like the Seminoles had to have cattle on it. Miccosukees had to turn it down. The older people did not want to accept anything from anybody, particularly the government.

The reason I believe we always felt that way is because we were taught not to work with the U.S. government in those things. We grew up with it and felt like we were doing something wrong when we sat down just like I'm talking to you about something. But it was worse when you worked with the U.S. government, particularly back in the 1950s. So you felt like you gave yourself away and you gave away some things, and you were taught not to do that. That's the only thing we had a problem with.

I think I said over and over and over to the people, we were told not to set up a reservation; don't think about having a reservation; don't live on a reservation; but now people were thinking we should have a reservation to survive. That's what people were thinking. And some traditional people out there still didn't want the reservation; they believed they might have to pay some property taxes and things like that. I didn't know what was the best thing for the people about having a reservation; if you know what you are doing, the government says this is your land. People know exactly what *reservation* means. But to us they take away other lands that belong to you; you have no rights. If you go outside the reservation, you have to pay tax, and do this, and this, and the white man's way. That seems to be the second step, to try and convince our people because they're dead against it, especially the traditional people I worked with; they were so against any reservation. I had a hard time trying to help them learn to be a little more flexible so we can have some reservation land. They didn't want that, but in the long run you find them all on the reservation. So I guess our judgment might have been pretty bad at that time. We thought maybe we were making a big mistake, but I think, to me, we did right. Because like it or not, you found your elders telling you not to do those things, but the same ones end up on the reservation. I don't know if they realized what they were doing, but it happened.

I always told my people that we were always taught not to be on a reservation, not to take anything from the white man, because they always turn around and say, "I give you this; now I want the whole thing." Like we were talking about the payment from the United States for taking land away from the Seminoles and Miccosukees years ago—the Seminole Tribe wanted to get payment from them. And we didn't like them because they were doing that. We were not looking at that particular land. We've been taught that the U.S. government gives you so many dollars, not very much, but they're going to take all the land away from you by right. We're not taking money, but if we took money, they write down your name and file it, then they pay you off later not for that particular reservation but for the whole state of Florida. That's what we were taught—be careful—and it's true.

That's what the Seminoles did; that's why we did not like them for a long time. And we still think that it is wrong. You're not supposed to take that money. I believe the [Indian Claims Commission] money the Seminoles took, our share is still in that trust fund some way. So we kept telling the people not to take that money because the minute you take it, people will look at us differently.

I don't know if you know or not, people are looking at us today as if we are not conquered yet just because we never took that money. We thought, too, people would take it and spend it and be worse off. We were not going to do that.

There used to be a Seminole reservation that was south of the Tamiami Trail. It is part of the Everglades National Park now because the park took over the land that had been a state reservation. Some of the people there were already moving around, but the land out there was supposed to be an Indian reservation. The government wanted to take that reservation land in the Everglades and put aside other land someplace else for a reservation. Some of the elders probably dealt with the government, and the government went ahead and put them on the Alligator Alley [Interstate 75] reservation. Those were the types of things the government and people were always doing to the Indians. The Indian had no say. They did not have a chance to say, "I want it this way," or "I would like to see it done this way," or to even say that they agreed. People were just going to do what they thought was good for the Indians. Those kinds of things used to happen often.

Years ago the government worked with the Miccosukees and Seminoles together and did not want to split the two tribes. The government wanted to recognize one tribe and have a reservation just for one tribe. That had been going on for years. Our people did not want to live on the government reservation and deal with the government, so it took us a long time to get where we are today. That is why there are two tribes, the Seminole Tribe of

Florida and the Miccosukee Tribe of Indians of Florida, with their own constitutions and bylaws. That is the way it ought to be because they have their own way of doing things. They have their language, and we have our own language, *Eelapone*. The United States government did not want to do it, but we forced them to allow us separate constitutions.

There were many Miccosukee people living in the Everglades area in the 1950s. Their families lived on islands. Some of them had gift shops and lived along the Tamiami Trail, where a few of them still live today. Different families did pretty well by doing that. Government agents have been down here for many years and had different offices. One office was established in the Hollywood area many years ago. Miccosukees called that agency office Big City [the old Indian name for the site was Big City Island]. Government agents were always watching what Miccosukees did. Miccosukees did not like the agents even though they always said they were there to give the Indians a hand and help out.

Miccosukees had learned not to trust white people and thought they are all the same way because their skin is alike, white skin. A government agent might have been a nice person. Regardless, he was automatically considered a "bad guy" because at one time white people were enemies. For years they killed many of our people. They sent our people to Oklahoma, and on the way many families and children died. This is the reason Miccosukees do not care for the government. Our people lived by themselves on big hammocks in the Glades area for many years after the wars, hiding from soldiers and everybody else. They hunted, fished, and did what they had to do to live. They did it well.

Miccosukee leaders met with Seminole leaders. The Seminoles had asked the Miccosukees if they wanted to be part of their tribe before they organized the Seminole Tribe. Miccosukee leaders said that they did not want to join them. The Seminole Tribe of Florida was organized, and they established a constitution and bylaws. It took a lot of time and work. Their federal reservations were already established at Hollywood, Brighton, and on Big Cypress. They had a big responsibility to operate under their constitution at that time. Miccosukees did not want to be under the Seminole constitution. The superintendent of the tribe was surprised that the Miccosukees did not join the Seminoles.

The Termination Hearings

We were already trying to work with Eisenhower, who was president at that time, not really working with him but we wanted him to understand our feelings. We wanted to make sure that the Indian Bureau and government in Washington listened to us and understood how our feelings are for Miccosukee people.

So I didn't have an easy job.

We found out that we had to go to Washington, but before that I had to get some type of help like a lawyer that understood that type of business because I was just a young guy who didn't know too much of anything. In fact, I didn't know the Bureau of Indian Affairs was in Washington. But our leaders, those people we call medicine men, they had selected us to go up there and make sure that nothing happened to us. In other words, we were not asking for anything.

We were not telling the government what we wanted; we didn't want anything from them. That was my job: to let them know we were not too concerned about education and welfare and all the things that tribal reservation people usually had to work with. We didn't have a reservation; we never wanted it. We really didn't care about that type of life at that particular time. The medicine men who selected me to speak for them were so particular about not taking anything from the white man, not even ten cents, and not accepting anything from them. So I'd always go back and tell them this is what Washington wants us to do. If they said yes, we could do it, I would say yes. In other words, I was taking strict orders.

So this particular time [1954], when termination was supposed to be taking place in Washington, we didn't really know what it was, but the lawyer Morton Silver tried to explain to us what it meant. But it looked like we had to go, and we didn't have any funds for that type of business. To get enough money for us to buy tickets on a train, what the people did was everybody put a couple of dollars together here and there, and we had enough money to send people up there and had enough for food and a hotel room. At that particular time it was cold in D.C., but I went and Jimmy Billie went, and George Osceola, an elderly man who was barefoot and wore long skirts; we went dressed like we were here! So anyhow, the three of us and Morton Silver our lawyer, four of us altogether, we went up there on the train and spent a couple of days there. Meantime, we talked to many, many reporters and different people. We tried to bring a message to Eisenhower; my medicine people told me to tell Eisenhower, to let him know we didn't really care what he had done. We didn't care what he's got; we didn't want anything from him.

We just wanted to live our life. We just wanted to live on the land the way we had always lived on it—to hunt and find food the way we had always done it. We didn't want anything new, any new ideas; we didn't want that. So that's what made us want to go up there.

When we got there, it sounded different. But we realized what it was; we realized that the reservation people happened to be there. The Seminole Tribe and lots of Indian people were there. Some attorneys were there from different tribes. Some of the senators up there we recognized from here in the state of Florida. Senator [George] Smathers and Congressman [James] Haley from Sarasota were there, and they kind of sympathized with us be-

Fig. 7. Jimmie Billie, Buffalo Tiger, George Osceola, and Morton Silver examine the Buckskin Declaration before leaving for the Washington DC termination hearings in 1954. Courtesy of the Historical Museum of Southern Florida, Miami.

cause we all got along good down here and never caused any trouble for anybody, so they respected us for being there. But they didn't know why we were there. Just like we didn't know why we were there; but once we got there, we realized it was a good thing we came up. But when we testified on that subject [termination] and they asked us what to do, we didn't accept the idea or reject it; we just said we didn't want anything from the white man's government.

I guess that did it. So the senators and congressmen who were in charge of the committees agreed they were just going to let it go and not push [termination]. The Buckskin Declaration we took up and gave to some person; the president's aide, I believe; he took it. We gave it to him and explained what it means. They could read it; that's what we said; anybody can read it. I used to have a copy, but everything I had burned up. After that we felt like we had accomplished something, so we didn't feel bad and we came home.

The Struggle Continues

But we had other problems too. It didn't have to be just the government doing something to Indian people. The reservation people at Hollywood and Big Cypress and Brighton, those were established reservations, and we didn't have any reservation down here. The land we hunted and lived on many, many years—we thought that belonged to us.

In 1957 the Seminoles organized themselves with a constitution and by-laws approved by the government and wanted us to come in with them; our people still said no. But they had some people like my cousin—I hate to say this—Mike Osceola, who wanted to be the representative from here. So he got himself elected and was supposed to represent us up there. But we were still fighting and didn't want to go and be part of the Seminole Tribe.

You have to recognize at that particular time we met so many times with some people from Okeechobee: Sam Jones and Oscar Holt and those medicine people came down. They were good friends with Ingraham Billie since they were all medicine men. They talked about what rights they had up there and what rights we had down here, and they recognized that we had always been that way; we had different languages and ate different foods, so there was no problem that we didn't belong to that tribe. But we didn't have much experience like we have today. We could have done something different at that time, I guess, but we didn't; we just fought them. We told the government and Bureau of Indian Affairs that we didn't belong to the Seminole Tribe. We tried to stay away from Seminole Tribe, but people were still trying to get us involved with the Seminole Tribe.

Then we started doing things like going to Washington and different places and trying to tell other nations—the only place we didn't go was to the Russian embassy. A number of other countries recognized we had a problem. Mexico and France recognized our problem, and then later the Cubans seemed to recognize our problem too.

It's hard to say who had the idea of going to Cuba. I was talking about what happened when the Creeks Oscar Holt and Sam Jones came down and talked to us, lots of talking, about what happened years ago, what type of people were here. Like the French were here, the British were here, the Spanish were here, and they knew about all those things. And they said we had signed a treaty with those people, British and Spanish. Where are they? That's what Morton Silver was supposed to be finding. We found them; it took a long time. We found some of them in Spain, and some came from England. So we had them and realized we had been treated okay for that time, so we wanted to get help from them. That's how we started.

When we started doing that, we got involved with different people like the Cubans. We can sit here today and that kind of stuff is not so important, but years ago, let's say back in the 1950s and 1960s, Communism was a big deal; it was like poison. So that's what people started calling Morton Silver and some of the lawyers we worked with. Then we got to be called Communists, too; we were Communists—okay? We didn't care because we knew what we were talking about ourselves. When that kind of thing came up, things got tough. In other words, when we got rolling a little bit, when we were getting bigger and had more power, newspapers and everybody seemed to know [about our involvement with Cuba].

Then Morton Silver said, "I'm not getting paid." Okay, he never got paid; I never got paid. But he said, "That's all right. Maybe one day you will get your land, then maybe you can share a piece of it with me." I think he did it in writing. That's when the congressmen and senators, especially the committee, came down with James Haley to investigate. They thought we were mixed up with the Communists and Morton Silver was the one who put us into that, and he wanted to go ahead and put a reservation in our name and get a piece of land to get paid for that. So that's why they came down investigating us.

But when they came down here, we told them—we said it over and over and over—we are not Seminoles; we live a different life down here. We don't want anything from anybody. This is the way it is in the Glades; we always lived that way and wanted that life. At that particular time some of the congressmen made it pretty hard on us because some white folks who stood up and tried to help us antagonized those people, and there were some strong words back and forth. I think our side never got upset about it, but you know how senators and congressmen can blast you! That's when we went to Cuba.

Another problem we had was with the state of Florida. They were trying to work with us too, but when Governor [LeRoy] Collins was in control of the state of Florida, he set up a watch committee to investigate Seminoles and Miccosukees again. Louis Capron [an avocational historian who wrote on Florida Indian culture] was on that committee. They did that to us, too [investigated accusations of Communist influence]. But those people never said anything about me as an individual; they were only talking about the groups. They said the Miccosukees were separate from the Seminoles; they had their own life and should be treated that way. Morton Silver thought because they were not working with us, that was not good. Collins did say he would like to set up a reservation land out in the Glades for Miccosukees, but the U.S. Indian commissioner, Glenn Emmons, turned it down. He said he couldn't do that because the president wanted to terminate reservations, so he would be working against him, and he couldn't do that. So that's what happened.

Meeting Castro

We did meet [Fidel] Castro. What they did was give us places to go and do different things. We didn't see him much, except one time he made a little speech. About two or three Castros were there. It was hard to tell which one was the real Castro. It looked like they had doubles for him; it was pretty hard to tell which was the real one. He was big and said hello to us and that kind of thing. I think they made a lot of pictures there, too, but I don't have any. Here again, it looked like it was planned and everything was set up. You just got in to see him—come and go quickly. That's what he was doing.

I remember the things he had to say. He said—I guess, because the in-

Fig. 8. Governor LeRoy Collins of Florida and Buffalo Tiger, ca. 1957. Courtesy of Buffalo Tiger.

terpreters said—"We are your friends, and we're going to help you all we can." He promised us that if we had a hard time living in the United States, our homeland, then Cuba was open for us any time. Yes, he made an offer, but through interpreters. But that's the only thing I remember when we really faced him.

The other times, I believe the next day, he made a speech for one whole afternoon. We had to go way high, really high up there [in the stadium] to see him. He's up there [on stage] with his group and made a speech, and we were guests, so we went there. We were sitting outside. I thought it was very hot, and you got thirsty! Hot sun, hot day, I had to bear with it! Anyhow, everything went okay. We came down and went back to the hotel and rested. Well, I don't see how he could talk that long!

Fig. 9. Miccosukee delegation arrives in Cuba, 1959. *Standing left to right:* Morton Silver, Howard Osceola, a Cuban soldier, Tiger Tiger, Buffalo Tiger, a Cuban soldier, John Osceola, Homer Osceola, Raymond Tiger Tail. *Kneeling left to right:* Wild Bill Osceola, Calvin Sanders, John Willie, Stanley Frank. Courtesy of the Historical Museum of Southern Florida, Miami.

I believe, businesswise, we were there about three days. All together it will be about four days. Let me tell you, you had a lot of Americans and newspapers there. One newspaper reporter from here, the *Miami Herald*, he went with us. He was a friend. He wanted to go, so we took him. He was Jane Reno's son, Bobby Reno; I think she's got two sons. He took some pictures, and when he got back he put us on the front page.

It didn't take long before I had phone calls. That's when the state began calling me to talk: We have a reservation, and you know we're going to work things out, and you're not going to go back anymore. Of course, I couldn't change anything then. Max Denton [state Indian commissioner] called first. And he promised me there was going to be a reservation set up to what we wanted and that kind of thing. I told him we would get together. The same afternoon I had a call from Washington. They asked me to promise not to go back and not to talk to those people again, and they were going to come down and work with us. I told them yes, we'd be happy to talk to them, so they were going to have a representative come down. He was going to investigate our situation and the other group Morton Silver was working with.

Reginald Miller, he's part Indian, was the guy who came down to investigate the situation. Miller was the most qualified person in the Bureau of Indian Affairs working with recognition. He said we would have to have an election. So he spent maybe a month investigating and checking back and forth all the time. But he wanted to give Morton Silver a lot of time to find whether his group had a legal right to recognition. The government indicated that the majority of our people were trying to do the right thing to be recognized because we had the materials.

That is what we were trying to do when we moved the Miccosukee headquarters to the *Chickeechobee* [on the Tamiami Trail]. We had an election so the majority of the people could go for it or oppose it. I had that vote result. So they checked and said your people are trying to do the right thing, so they used that information. That's what Miller tried to find from the other group, but Morton Silver did not supply information. It was just not clear cut: there seemed to be lots of back and forth. Morton Silver was on the opposite side rather than working it out with us. We talked about that so many times; we could have just worked together and gone through the whole thing, but it did not happen that way.

By this time Mrs. LaVerne Madigan [representing the American Association on Indian Affairs] had been talking with us, and Mr. Arthur Lazarus [Washington attorney for the AAIA] was behind us now. Then some of the Washington staff of the Bureau of Indian Affairs got behind us and the whole idea. Even the Seminole Tribe members changed their minds. Before, they just wanted us to be under one tribe with them. Then the investigation recognized we were qualified to be a tribe. There was so much work we had to do, like draw up a constitution and program for school, law enforcement, and other things, until we had elections.

Our Tribal Name

We really didn't have a clear-cut understanding of the [meaning of the] Miccosukee Tribe yet. We did ask *Cheeshaponke* spiritual leader Oscar Holt and the *Eelaponke* medicine man Ingraham Billie what is the meaning in *Eelapone*. We thought the language was coming from many [elements] together. Maybe the Spanish used it somehow; it looked like that happened. Meantime, we spelled it differently. When we talked about this, we spelled it differently. My brother Jimmy used to know pretty well because we sat and talked about this thing during council meeting—I'm talking about traditional council meeting. They talked with Oscar Holt and Sam Jones and Ingraham Billie, trying to come up with something clear-cut.

They said we used to be called so many times *mikosukee*—it sounded something like that. Then after we decided how Miccosukee should be spelled, Morton Silver got into it. He jotted it out: "This is what you're saying, and I'll ask those medicine people if this is what they're saying." They said it's all right, it's good enough, so we started using that. So that's what Miccosukee came from. *Mikosukee*, it seems to be old language. *Miko*, it means something like the head; I don't mean like your and my head, but something bigger [a leader]. *Sukee* is pig or hog. We had an idea maybe one time people used [the word] to mean either of two things: either the clan or those people who managed the hogs, either of those two. When the bureau came down, we played with how it should be [spelled]. But the name *Miccosukee*, it was decided before that. To me, that's clear cut, but you have to know where it came from.

Our Tribal Constitution

The constitution, we really did not know too much about it. What did it mean? But Reginald Miller had suggested that we had to have a constitution and bylaws so we would be organized under that and the Bureau of Indian Affairs would recognize it. A gentleman named Rex Quinn, he's an Indian and an expert in Indian constitutions, came down to work with us. He had worked with Seminole Tribe and a few other tribes. So we did that.

Let me tell you about how we did it. It was not easy.

First we had to select members of my people who were going to be on the committee. I happened to be one, and my brother Jimmy Tiger, and

John Poole, and I believe Sonny Billie, John Willie, and George Osceola. The constitution, we understood, was going to protect our people immediately, and Quinn pointed out to us there were so many ways we could do it. He wanted to know if we wanted to go ahead and detail everything we wanted to do.

I talked to my committee, and they asked what did I think? I said, "I don't think we need all of it. We're going to grow; we are a little tribe; we do what we can with it now, and maybe we can add to it later."

He said, "You want a frame for the constitution and add meat and fat later?"

I said, "Yes, it's a better idea if we don't finish now and later we have to change so much. We don't want to do that; we'll just go ahead and take what we've got and do changes later."

He said, "You can do that."

So we started working in that way, and he did ask so many questions. Let's take the Business Council. We could have had a tribal council to run the tribe, and the Business Council would run the business. We said we really don't want to go that way because we were such a small tribe, and we would have two sets of powers there, and it's not going to work for us. So let's go ahead and have the Business Council run business and take care of the reservation and protect the people, and the tribal people would continue to live like at the Green Corn Dance. So we left it with the Business Council running the day-to-day business on the reservation, but religious practices should be left to the people the way it's always been.

Why is there a constitutional requirement that four or more clans—but the minimum is four—must be represented for the General Council to [make broad decisions]? We did it because that's the way we always ran our customs. It's part of our life; that had to be there. Today we are glad that's the way it is.

When you organize yourself to live on reservation, what you like to have on the reservation is law. So many laws. But what are you going to do with those laws? We were talking about that, too. We were not talking about having experiences [such as crime] like we have today. It was a simple life we lived at that time—the only life we knew. But they did say to us, sooner or later you will be running into problems so you have to put something in it on how to protect your people on the reservation. So we did do what we had to do at that time, knowing we were going to make some changes.

Everything we were talking about at that time, it is possible we might have to add more meat. The frame was already done so we just added whatever we wanted to make it better.

They asked, "Do you want alcohol on the reservation?" And we said, "No." "Do you want gambling on the reservation?" Our people said, "No, no gambling on the reservation." I'm talking about gambling to make money. They said some tribes do different things, like it or not, like the girls want to sell themselves on the reservation. We said, "No, that's not going to happen." So many things they suggested, and our people said no.

One thing I remember: we did not agree to have state law step in and take care of us. It never happened. If there were any reservation problems, the federal [authorities] would be looking after the people, investigating, health, and all that.

One big thing, I thought and we thought, we knew some of these people in charge of the Green Corn Dance—what we call the medicine men—we knew they wanted to practice the way they always had. So that's why we left them to not be included. Our people have traditions that they have to practice, but the Business Council had nothing to do with that. In other words, they can't say we are here to take care of [religious affairs] for you; they can't do that.

Another problem we ran into was how were we going to handle it in case some people go outside for marriage. We had it easy because Rex Quinn had experience—he was good for that job—and he suggested to us that outside marriage usually happened. So we fished around in knowing what we needed to say. This time we were talking about outside marriage and having the youngsters be members. We could only go just half-blood, no less; just half-blood would be accepted. Either husband, wife, or child of a half-blood Miccosukee can come into our tribe, but not those that come from other places. Let's say two Seminoles—even though they look like they belong to us, they are Seminoles—maybe they are speaking Miccosukee same as Miccosukee people, but today they belong to Seminole Tribe. We have to treat them like where they belong, so they are not qualified to be where we are. It's not really fair, but that's the way the constitution is already drawn up. Only Miccosukee members have to be half-blood; could be black, could be Spanish, could be anybody, but has to be half Miccosukee blood. We have a problem with it now, but it's still practiced as we did in the beginning.

As far as having rules about what Miccosukee people must do on the reservation, we did not indicate it too much because it was going to come
later. We said maybe one day we need to have an extra council from the traditional area. We didn't say that, we left it out, but we will get ready to establish that if we need it. Otherwise we are still going the way we are now.
But sometimes I feel like the tribe needs somebody; they don't have to be
power people, but somebody who will keep language and culture and all
that. We left it out, but someday we will be talking about that.

We have the lawmaker in traditional ways, too, but it is different in the
constitution. Only that particular person is selected like that; the office is
only good during the meetings. He's for controlling people during the
meeting. If you are out of line, get back in line. If we are talking about
something and someone is half-drunk and running his mouth, he will be
thrown out. A sergeant-at-arms, that's what he is; not a lawmaker. I have
to tell the people all the time; they look at him that way, but that's not what
it meant. That seems to be a problem now, too, so we have to make some
corrections.

Were we trying to have a minimal government? Exactly! Yes, I think it
was good enough for that particular time. Knowing we were not experienced in the white man's way in 1952, '53, '54, we used our own traditional way. We always used that way; we still use it today, but it is not getting stronger. I don't think the Business Council has the power to do that
either. So I've been thinking we ought to look at it.

Today we might need something stronger to control what's going on
here now. Like I just finished saying, we are not supposed to have gambling on the reservation, okay? The situation we are in now, even though
we are a reservation, it was set up strictly for that [gambling]. The people's
reservation looks like a business reservation. That's what we have now. But
nobody ever says that. I'm talking about the gambling place; it's different.
I know that; I was still in office, and we had to take that out and put it
someplace else because we said we are not going to have gambling on the
reservation. [The Miccosukee Resort and Convention Center is located on Krome Avenue, west of Miami.] Not only that, we feel like all the things people believe
in—I'm talking about traditional people—they would be lost so quickly
when so many people come and spend their money, have a good time, and
enjoy themselves; it will kill the culture we have right away. So let's take
gambling out and put it someplace else. So it was done that way, but we

never said why. That's the only thing I said—and I don't think many people believed me.

Only forty-one people voted to accept the constitution. Very few people voted because they didn't want it. Even the interested ones, people told them not to vote, okay? It was not easy. We had people opposing it hanging around all over; they don't let them get that vote. My wife [Phoebe] was with us all the time taking notes. Most of the people didn't want to be bothered. That's the way it is now. People say, "We don't have to fool with that." The Business Council is running everything.

Rex Quinn was good to us. I don't know how the Seminoles see it, but with us he was okay. He would suggest this can be done, this can be done, this can be done, and you just had to tell him what you wanted to go with: "Any ideas of your own, just tell me." He was very open; he was not force-ful; he really wanted to do something. But let me tell you, the constitution we have, to me, is the best anybody can have. I can say that because we have looked at it so many times. We can change it, we can add to it, but people right now, they don't want to make any changes yet. Maybe one day they will, but the only thing I say—and we said it during the time—maybe we need to have two sets of councils with the traditional people having their own setup. Today I see they need that. I don't think we had any major changes to the constitution while I was in office. There were a few ordi-nances when I was in office, but the constitution remains basically the same.

THE MICCOSUKEE TRIBE

The Miccosukee Tribe of Indians of Florida received official recognition from the federal government in 1962, and Buffalo Tiger was elected its first tribal chairman. The new tribe had neither land of its own nor a regular source of income, however. Initially, the nascent tribal government was dependent on loans from the Bureau of Indian Affairs and occasional payments from the state of Florida for grazing rights or oil exploration leases. Great Society programs were established for the tribe during the 1960s, but they provided minimal employment opportunities. Education and health care programs for the Miccosukees became a major concern for tribal leaders; funds were difficult to obtain, however, and remained tightly controlled by the local BIA superintendent. Then in 1970 President Nixon announced a new federal policy of Indian self-determination under which tribes could control their own affairs. The Miccosukees seized the moment and, despite resistance from conservative elements within the BIA, became the first Indian tribe to sign a comprehensive contract with the federal government. The Miccosukee Agency was closed, and the tribal Business Council took operational control of all services for the people, placing the tribe in the vanguard of the Indian self-determination movement. Here Buffalo Tiger explains the efforts to achieve political and financial security for his people, as well as his own goals and aspirations as a modern tribal leader.

Living with a Constitution

There were Indian leaders who had been with the Miccosukees at first, but they decided to join the Seminole Tribe. Miccosukee leaders knew they had to go on and finish the work that had to be done. They had something going and knew that they could not quit, giving in to those who had caused them trouble before. Miccosukees are not supposed to live on a reservation like they do now. But the leaders recognized that the constitution would not be effective if they did not live on a reservation where the laws could be enforced and the people could be protected. Miccosukees would be under state or county laws and have no protection without the laws of their own constitution. The constitution protects the reservation, the traditional Green Corn Dance ground, and the Green Corn Ceremony.

Indians are supposed to fight to protect their traditional practices, religion, and language. Miccosukee leaders made those decisions for the young people in 1963–65, knowing that they would have to go to school and learn Miccosukee and English together and that they could play games and sports. They wanted a better life for the younger people. Things were changing, and Miccosukees wanted a better life for themselves. They recognized that they needed guidance to teach the people how to make their life better and healthier. They also realized that they should build a way of life for themselves and should not have to make it entirely like the white man's way. Some white man's ways can be blended with the Indian ways.

Tribal Businesses

After we got a constitution, they paid me a hundred dollars a week. We didn't have money so the bureau managed to get some organization to donate money to help pay for my groceries. We turned around and borrowed money from the Bureau of Indian Affairs—I think it was about seventy-five thousand dollars, something like that—to develop a gasoline station and Indian restaurant. We did that and spent a lot of time to get that finished. Then we had to get my people working. They wanted to work, but we didn't know how to do things like people do in the city. So we talked about how to handle that. We talked to the county, and they said they would be happy to supply some experts in restaurant management. Then my wife and people like that helped inside, so when we got the restaurant open it

Fig. 10. Buffalo Tiger as chairman of the Miccosukee Tribe, 1970s. Courtesy of Buffalo Tiger.

was very nice and the people were happy to work there. We got some Seminoles to come down, like Marie Osceola, to work with us as a waitress. We had a couple of Miccosukee girls working as waitresses so we can learn how. My wife Phoebe kind of watched everything in the restaurant, helped manage it. Of course she didn't get paid! As far as the county, the expert taught us how to keep books, how to do wages and checks; that is how they helped us out. The other thing—what kind of checks to do for customers—we had to go to school for. I learned something from them, and [current tribal chairman] Billy Cypress—at that time he was a young boy—he was there too, learning how to work in the restaurant. Some Miccosukee boys used to be there. But we had to get an expert to cook, a real cook, not Miccosukee. But later we got some Indian ladies to start helping in the kitchen; they learned fast, so Miccosukees started cooking in that restaurant for a long time.

Miccosukee Tourist Village

The village on the Tamiami Trail was established by one elder man, my uncle Frank Willie. He was living there with his wife, but his wife did not want to stay. So Frank Willie stayed there. He had a little place, one sleeping *chickee* and one little cooking *chickee*; he also had a little island, a very small island there. And one little gift shop he put up because most of the families used to do that. He used to buy things and make different things to sell. Before that people like Smallpox Tommie and his wife, Jesse Willie, and Sam Willie and those people, even Jimmy Tommie, used to have a little farm in the Everglades before the Everglades National Park. And they had things going on there like farming areas and maybe a second camp so they could go in there to spend a couple of days. I'm not sure how many days they spent out there. This was before it was a national park.

So Frank Willie established a little camp, and for some reason he stayed. And Jimmy Tiger had a little camp just on the other side of the canal, the north side close to where Mary Osceola's camp is now.

That particular time Jimmy Tiger had lost his wife. Frank Willie thought he was getting older and his wife had left his place. So Frank Willie thought he should turn over his camp because Jimmy Tiger had to get out of his camp and go to another place anyhow. He was his uncle; Frank Willie was Bird clan, and Jimmy Tiger was a Bird clan. So Frank Willie told Jimmy Tiger he could have his place; it was not very much, but he could make something out of it. Jimmy Tiger must have been listening to that, so he took it. He put up more *chickees* on more land and put up a bigger store. Goes on and on each time, each year he added more fill and it got bigger and more *chickees*. That time [1960s] it belonged to Jimmy Tiger. That time he was married to a lady in the same clan as his first wife; everything seemed to be okay for him so they lived there for a long time.

He bought a lot of different things, crafts that people wanted to sell. We put in a little museum in the back—very small, but I always had the idea that I would like to have a museum. I did ask Jimmy Tiger could we do it, and he agreed he was going to help. So we did that. That time I was working with the elders; I was representing them. I did not have a job or funds to buy gas and to do the things I had to do. So they thought it was a good idea for me to have a museum and I would get a little money out of it. So we started that way. Everything went okay.

Jimmy Tiger thought he was getting older and he could not take care of the village and wanted to go ahead and sell the village to the tribe. This was discussed over and over and over, not just one year but so many times. And people made up their minds we didn't have money to buy it. But we promised him we would pay him as soon as we got some money, and we would pay him all along. And he agreed to do that, sell it to the tribe. So he said we could pay him later. I guess we got it on credit. We took it and started running it. We owed the money to Jimmy Tiger until we got funds from the state and that time we paid him off. Also, we bought his airboat operation; he had a big airboat operation at that time. So we paid him off. We were not in debt at that time.

The Big Chickee

Later people decided that we should have the council meeting building; we call it *Chickeechobee*. So we built a big *chickee*, and everybody thought it was a good idea. So we built it across away from Jimmy Tiger's camp, just on the north side of a small canal at that time. Further north was a big fill there, so we put a big *chickee*, a nice one, on top of that. We had our council meetings there all the time.

And during that time everybody was a real Miccosukee—everybody was speaking their own language, and they went to find food out in the Everglades; they were still planting corn and different things like that—really still traditional people. And I remember everyone speaking their own language; they just could not speak English. And really, when the council was meeting, nobody took notes. We did that in traditional ways, and when we talked we agreed to do things [by consensus].

Today people might think we didn't have anything, that we did not do anything. But we did a lot of work by just words and we agreed to do it, and we do those things. That was the way traditional people were always doing. Everything seemed to be going well for us, the Miccosukee people. We kept our traditional feeling and traditional language, all that should be practiced all the time every day.

One day the Corps of Engineers wanted to put in a bigger canal in that area. We didn't agree with them. We had a lot of meetings. They asked us to tear the *chickee* down. They said they would dynamite to blow up coral rock to make the canal bigger. We didn't want that. We had to fight back. It was about thirty-five to forty feet or maybe fifty feet, I'm not sure. Another canal, a bigger one, and they were going to put in a road like we have now. Back in 1962 or '63, we really didn't want that to happen; we wanted to keep our *chickee* there. We thought it was not hurting anything, and we should keep it there. But they wanted us to move it [for the road], but I see today it was not so. [The road] was way away from where we had that *chickee*. It was not too far away from the old canal, not too far away from the village we have there now. So really they just wanted us to tear it down, and we knew it at that time, so we were right. I can see now. Even though they wanted us to tear it down, we did not want to tear it down; we wanted to fight. We kept that *chickee* there, and they could not come through. But they would not let us do that. They just told us that the dynamite would destroy the *chickee*.

We moved the *chickee*, and they gave us a little money to build another one. So now we had a *chickee* north of that dike. We spent a lot of time talking to Water Management and Corps of Engineers and all that. I believe we used to meet with Fresh Water Fish and Game Commission also. We had big meetings so many times, but we never gave in. We always tried to stick with what we thought was right to keep what we had.

Health Care

Earlier, before the tribe was organized, we had not reached modern medicine to treat sickness. We did not speak English; we did not know how to
talk to a doctor or white man. Miccosukees would get sick with colds, ane-
mia, and parasites. We had water problems because we drank well water.
We did not want anything from the U.S. government. At that particular
time, health care money was available through the Bureau of Indian Affairs, but their offices were in Oklahoma City. Someone would leave as-
pirin or other medicines, but we would not see a doctor. We took care of
ourselves and did our own things. We [Tiger's family] went to a medical
doctor ourselves; his name was Dr. Reintz. Somehow someone was paying
for that. We did not know the money was sitting there all the time. After a
while we realized there was health care money set up for Miccosukees and
Seminoles. When we went to a doctor or hospital for care, they would call
it a welfare program. We learned that the Indian Health Service (IHS) and
Bureau of Indian Affairs finally set up health care money through Tallahassee. We still experienced problems. IHS and BIA did not do a good job.

At the same time, the Seminole Tribe already had a health care service.
They got more help because they had the BIA superintendent on their reservation. Miccosukees got together with Joe Dan Osceola and [other] leaders from the Seminole Tribe and made a request to IHS and Washington to
have health funds transferred to an individual in Jacksonville. Dr. Johnson,
IHS national director, answered by helping us.

In 1962 we organized, and health concerns were an important part in
the development of the constitution and bylaws. After we received federal
recognition, people started listening to us. We continuously wanted better
services for Miccosukees. We did not have a health care operation yet. So to
help us get things started, Reginald Miller, BIA superintendent [of the
Miccosukee Agency], arranged a meeting with the University of Miami and
several Dade County doctors and a hospital to make an arrangement on the
type of health care services that could be provided to Miccosukees. We
made a deal they would conduct a survey on Miccosukees to determine the
type of blood we had and the type of sicknesses we had. The tribe hardly
had anything. They provided a small trailer set up by the little school. The
trailer had medical equipment and doctors. They came for two days to take
blood tests. The results showed that we had a high rate of parasites, ane-

mia, and arthritis, and a few people had weak hearts. The doctors realized that we qualified for more health care. It qualified us to receive help from Indian Health Service. Dr. Johnson, IHS national director, came down to review our health concerns. When we started Indian health care, we knew what types of sicknesses people had.

After the survey and the tribe was working with Indian Health Service, we started working on improving communications between hospitals and Miccosukee patients. Dr. Billy Reintz understood our concern that Miccosukee patients should have traditional medicine while under hospital care, and he notified some hospitals of our concerns. With Dr. Reintz's help we established an agreement with hospitals that any hospitalized Miccosukee could receive traditional medicines as needed during their stay.

As the years passed, we continued to find ways to improve our health care services. In 1968 the tribe joined United Southeastern Tribes, Inc. USET was organized as a foundation for various tribes to gain political power and lobby on issues such as health care. We began contracting BIA programs and administering program services and funds ourselves. We decided to push for the tribe to contract with IHS ourselves.

In the meantime, the tribe took matters into its own hands and proposed to build a community health clinic. To do this, we had meetings of the General Council. Some people opposed it; they were unhappy because Miccosukees should use traditional medicine. It was approved because the majority of people wanted it. Our funds were short so we had to borrow money from a bank for constructing a clinic. We got the loan on the tribe's collateral. By 1972 the tribe had constructed a small clinic. People needing health care could receive either modern medicine or traditional medicine for treatment of their illnesses.

We continued to update services to the community while pushing to contract our own quality health care program with IHS. In 1973 we requested support from member tribes of USET at a meeting down here. The tribe had to push for it single-handedly because the other tribes opposed the idea. Emmit York, Choctaw chairman, agreed with us that we could do it. We continued to push the idea. Finally, we had a meeting with IHS officials to negotiate. By 1974 IHS agreed to allow the tribe to contract an Indian Health Service program.

Today the Miccosukee Tribe continues to contract an Indian Health Service program. The process took many years to succeed. We started with nothing; we were on our own, but with consistent determination we established an entire health system by contracting with Indian Health Service and using tribal assets. Since 1986 all new health care development has been under Billy Cypress's leadership. Today the tribe is making a profit from its enterprises, and a large amount of the profit goes into the health care delivery program on a continuous basis.

Our School

Miccosukee leaders knew they were going against things they had been taught when we established the constitution and bylaws but realized that they had no choice. They had to turn against what the people had taught them before—not to go to school or accept the white man's ways. The government agreed to half a day of English and half a day of Miccosukee and noncompulsory education, so the people accepted that. The Miccosukee school was started on the reservation. As real Indians, Miccosukee leaders knew that they were not supposed to do what they were doing but felt they had no choice. Families had to decide who would go to school and who would practice traditional learning.

As far as a school in the [housing] development, you probably think it's been there all the time, but it was just swamp there at one time. After we talked to the BIA, they were going to give us help. They built a school and an office building and gymnasium, so the government paid for it. The government also paid for the fill, so we did not pay for that.

We didn't know too much about running the school or any business, and of course we didn't have any funds to do that. The bureau seemed to have funds to operate the school and pay the teachers and whatever. But we had a lot of concerns about how the school should work. Particularly my people —not me but my people—didn't want to see Miccosukee youngsters learning strictly English and never speaking their own language. We already had a few young Miccosukees who had gone to public schools here in Dade County, and they were already acting different from traditional people. So they used that example, saying we should be teaching youngsters when they are young in Miccosukee as much as we can. So we had a lot of arguments between the bureau and ourselves over how much of it is fair.

So we decided half a day in English, and Miccosukee the other half of the day; in other words, we split the day so it wouldn't just be learning English because we realize Miccosukees should keep their culture and language. So that was agreeable to my people, plus they didn't have to come in town on the bus and go back. If they got used to living in the city, maybe they wouldn't want to go back; they might want to live in the city. So it would be better to live [in the Indian community] and go to school there and for sure they would be Miccosukees. That's why we decided to have our Miccosukee School be half a day Miccosukee learning and half a day English learning.

By that time [1971] we were thinking we needed even some of the non-Indian people learning a little in our language. Our people should learn English, too, so everybody worked pretty well together—but knowing one day Miccosukees are going to take over the whole program, everything. Meantime, we had to let other people work running business, running everything for us; we had to learn and pick up from them. So that's the idea we had, particularly me.

I had told my people so many times: we had to learn how to take responsibility to have something going for us. That means you have got to work and to be responsible every day when you're supposed to work. So I said that as far as learning English and Miccosukee, Miccosukee should remain strong. The only way we could go from there was to have someone write the language. Miccosukees expressed a feeling for that so they could use it more in teaching in the classrooms. So that's how we developed some materials. I was pretty strong with it.

A Contract with the Government

As far as contracting the school and programs, not only the school but everything—self-determination, we called it—we had an idea that's what we were [eventually] going to do when we accepted the constitution and bylaws. We didn't want the bureau running our affairs. We didn't want the bureau telling us what to do. We were old enough, and we have been here long enough, so let us run it ourselves. If we make mistakes, then we make mistakes.

So I had my mind made up that's what I was going to be talking to the Bureau of Indian Affairs about. I did that, and they liked it. They liked the idea, but they had never done it. But they said, "You can try it; we'll let you try it, and if it works out okay, we can go from there."

The tribe decided to go ahead. Commissioner Louis Bruce—he is part Indian—approved that, and we both signed a contract agreement. We had a picture made at that time, so they must have a picture in the bureau somewhere. The paper I signed people called "buy Indian," and that's when we had to let the bureau people [at the Miccosukee Agency] know either they were going to be working for us or they could go to other reservations for a job if they wanted to. They had a chance to keep their office by working for us. They didn't want that. There used to be an office in Homestead, and the bureau said go ahead and take the furniture and everything there, and if the employees don't want to work with you, let them go back where they came from. And we did that; they closed down, and we took over.

But I knew exactly what we were going to do, so we had no problem picking up there. Don't think it was easy to decide how we were going to do it. It took me a long, long time, and I talked to different tribes and talked to different people, and nobody knew what to do or how to do it. Even John Adams [tribal planner], who used to work with us, and Bobo Dean [tribal attorney] came down to talk to us, but they didn't know how to do it because [direct contracting] had never been done before. Deciding what we wanted to do was the hardest thing because we had just come out of the woods!

I was always telling my people the bureau seems to think I'm only an Indian talking and I'm going to go back to the reservation and forget about it. So I talked to them [the BIA] and said this is what we plan to do. They told me, "Get yourself a resolution on exactly what you're planning," and I said, "Okay." I came back and thought about what we were going to do. I had to be the engineer myself; lawyers couldn't tell me what to do; nobody could tell me what to do; we had to do it ourselves. So we finished [writing] what we believed should happen and took it back. The lawyers helped us. We sent a copy to Commissioner Bruce, and he liked it and wanted to try it. I was attending a meeting with other tribes, so he called me in, and we signed that contract [in 1971]. But they never believed I was going to follow through! [They thought] I was going halfway and would forget about it or they were going to get me sidetracked. Not me, I'm not that tractable; that's how I got them. So I always remembered that how you get something done is stick with it and sooner or later you get it.

Everybody knows about contracting, but some tribes didn't want to do that. I didn't have it easy. Really, it was not easy. The Cherokees didn't want me to do it. The Choctaws didn't want it. The Seminoles didn't want it. Nobody wanted what I was doing. I didn't see how the other reservations like Cherokee and Choctaw and big tribes had the bureau running affairs for them; some of them liked it that way, but we didn't. We never lived under the bureau, and we didn't want it.

I used to tell my secretaries, "You know, one day we are going to be running our affairs; we don't have to have an agent down here."

[They would say,] "Oh, Mr. Tiger, how can you talk that way? How do you think you're going to do it?"

[I said,] "You just watch and see."

Local Struggles

In the beginning we wanted to be friendly with Dade County. Dade County people involved in that jetport setup [plan for a second Miami airport, in the Everglades] came and talked to us. It sounded good. They were going to develop the jetport, and the planes would set down, and a lot of people would come from Europe and different places. We could have good craft shops and sell everything we made. Sounded good.

So some of the people thought it was not a bad idea, even though they didn't like airplanes. But as far as having a few extra dollars, they thought maybe we should go along with it, but not quickly. So we kind of waited around; then we saw different things going on, and people talking about what they were planning to do, and it got to be too big. It got to be a very big thing they were talking about.

So when time came, so many people were opposing that; we were like that, too, because of what the jetport was going to do for us really. You were talking about dirty water, polluting not only the water but also the air and everything; we had to look at that too. We were changing our mind on the other side. In time we did that. So when people came down from NBC Channel 6 News [Miami], we had to make some announcement. We had to say there is no place for us to go because the national park is behind us and this is open, but it's going to be the jetport and all. It was going to be east of Fifty-Mile Bend. That did it. Then other people started coming along opposing it, and we worked with those people. [The plan for a jetport was subsequently dropped.]

As far as the Big Cypress Preserve situation, it was clean cut because Congressman [James] Haley from the state of Florida, who used to be chairman of the Indian subcommittee, he was a friend to us and used to talk to me about it. He ran into me one time and said, "Buffalo Tiger, it's your place to say something now before we pass a law, and we're getting ready to do that. If you want to help your people, you have to act."

I said, "How much time do I have?"

He said not much time was left.

So I talked to Bobo Dean about what I should do, and he told me pretty much, "As far as the language, I think you can't say too much more than to say as long as my people are using it farming, living, and Green Corn Dance—traditional use would be the word for it—that's what we should add on." At first they wanted to know how many camps; they wanted how many this, how many that. We said, "Right now forget it; go ahead and do it the way it is." We tried to go with that, too, after they set it up; words in the act allow for traditional use. The Green Corn Dance can still be held there, as I see it. Then if people want to live there the traditional way, they can hunt, farm, and fish there.

Tribal Housing

Miccosukees decided they could build houses with a different look. Even Miccosukees' businesses could be different, not entirely like businesses in the city. They could build a community without concrete buildings that would be attractive to the public. Miccosukees found that they did not have to copy exactly what white men are doing in the city. They could build a community that reflects the way that Indians like to live. They realized the danger of becoming like people who live in slums. Long ago the public criticized some tribes who ended up living in slums and warned us about that. We all knew about slums. New York has big slums that are bad places to live. Miccosukees do not want to live like that and want to be proud of their lifestyle. They also decided they should be thinking about ways of creating this kind of life for themselves. They learned that mistakes had been made before and that they could be avoided by asking questions.

As far as what you see now—the water tank, the water pump, and all that—we supplied water for the Miccosukee Reservation. I believe we got some money from the BIA and the Indian Health Service. In the beginning we did not have electricity on the reservation. [Transmission lines] went out quite a ways but I don't remember how far. I remember we had to pay them seventeen thousand dollars approximately. The government paid that; we did not pay that ourselves. We managed to get light and power to go through. Other people also used it.

Those are the kinds of things our young people should remember because they may think the Miccosukee Reservation has been there a long time. It would be better for them to know how it happened and how it began. These are the kinds of things that are important. Sometimes during school maybe in a school project they can think back and remember what happened that time. Because every ten years everything seems to be changed. And it's going to be so continuously. So you all need to know is what happened that time, what it is today, and what's going to happen in ten years from now.

The Lease Area and Federal Reservation

After we made a trip to Cuba, [officials] called me and wanted to go ahead and work with us. The state said it could set up some type of [leasehold] reservation, but to us it was not really a reservation. It was just the way they did it and would take it back in maybe twenty-five or thirty years. We knew that, so we didn't want to believe that unless some lawyers got in it and we had something we could really hold onto.

We said we would get together and discuss this. We had a state Indian commissioner [in the 1960s]; Max Denton was the first commissioner and Bill Kick the second. Meanwhile, the bureau had come down too. So they kind of worked together, the state and bureau. They never told us just exactly what the deal was, but I was not listening to the state too much because we played with them too much and nothing came up. I was working with this group of people called the American Association on Indian Affairs [AAIA] in New York. The executive director, Mrs. LaVerne Madigan, was helpful, very helpful. She died, and Bill Byler took over. They stepped in and tried to see that the reservation was set up right. Arthur Lazarus was the lawyer they worked with and Bobo Dean. They worked with the Bureau of Indian Affairs; I remember some of the guys that worked with them. They all put their heads together. We were making such a big noise about the land, they wanted to make sure that the area set out would be protected. Even that was not working . . . the state would like to come by and check the businesses we had, or give us a permit where we can have a little business, or we can pay this license—they called it a license reservation. We didn't want that; we wanted it to be a reservation.

So if you read the agreement, that's how Lazarus and Bobo Dean set it up. They said we would like a reservation—no license, no permit. They said that's what it had to be, so that's the kind of wording we wanted in there. And even though it is not strictly a reservation, it is strict enough that we can protect it and keep it. I told people it is not the best thing, but the state didn't want a reservation. With this we can negotiate the lease when the time comes. I've never seen any time limit on the lease, but it did say if the population in Dade County is so great that they wanted that area to be developed, they have to pay cash to my tribe to take it. But I don't know where I saw it. I hope it's in the lease agreement because that is what we thought it said.

Fig. 11. Meeting to celebrate the settlement of Miccosukee land claims, 1982. *Left to right:* Bobo Dean (Washington DC attorney), Adela Gonzalez (secretary to the Miami-Dade Mayor), Bob Mitchell (adviser to Buffalo Tiger), Bob Ferguson (friend of the Miccosukees), Buffalo Tiger, Joel Frank (Seminole Tribe officer), Arthur Lazarus (Washington DC attorney). Courtesy of Buffalo Tiger.

It took a lawsuit to put the State Indian Reservation into federal trust. My people didn't want to do that, but we had no choice. We had no money to pay for it either. That's why my people didn't want to go with me. But we finally worked with Bobo Dean and Mr. Lazarus to do the job, and we would find the money to pay. They didn't say how much—maybe they did, but I can't remember exactly how much they said they would charge us—to file suit. There was money involved in taking right-of-way [for Interstate 75 and a canal] on the reservation, so when we won the case there would be some money there they could take; so my people said yes, they could do that. So that's how we made a deal. I think we paid them almost one hundred thousand dollars total. It took them a long time to go to court and do different things. There were so many things we had to go through with it, not just one little reservation. It ended in 1982 with the act. [PL 97-399 *federalized the Miccosukee portion of the State Indian Reservation, established a 189,000-acre lease area, and confirmed the tribe's permit to its headquarters area on the Tamiami Trail.*]

No Longer Chairman

I lost the last election I had. I really don't know why, but it seems to be politics. No one told me what is really wrong, but the thing that convinced me was one of my nephews, my own blood, turned against me for some reason. He was an alcoholic, but he had influence with many young people because of drinking parties all night. They thought that a new guy, my brother-in-law Sonny Billie, who happened to be a medicine man, they thought maybe he was the guy who could get me out. I didn't know too much about it. I had my own things to do; I couldn't worry about it. My secretary, Alice Drake, kept telling me that so many people were listening to my nephew about kicking me out. I said, "Okay, if they are going to get me out, let them go ahead and vote to do that." So that's what happened.

I don't think Sonny knew what was really going on, but he should; he was my assistant chairman at one time. I always respected the guys who worked with me, but sometimes other people didn't feel that way. He was married to my sister, plus he was a medicine man, so he shouldn't have to do that. But he convinced a lot of young people, and my nephew was right in the middle of it. Before he died he said, "I made a mistake. I'm the guy that did it. I'm the guy that pushed him to do it, and Sonny pushed too

Fig. 12. Buffalo Tiger and his sons meet with King Juan Carlos and Queen Sofia of Spain during their 1982 visit. Courtesy of Buffalo Tiger.

hard. Now everything is messed up, so we're going to have to go back and get him out." Looks like that happened.

Was there resentment against my family? It could be, but there was nothing to that. Nobody got ahead. I didn't have money to pay for my own bills. And my sons had to work; they had jobs, but they were not getting rich at that. We continued to develop tourism. We went out of the country to South America, Spain, small countries, and small cities. We established friendships; they helped me do those things. We enjoyed those days.

It was politics, strictly politics. What they thought they could do, if Sonny could get in there, he could use heavy equipment to develop rock pits some way, sell rock to build roads, and use tribal funds. I do know that; he said that many times. He's in that type of business even today.

As far as people saying I was taking money, and doing this and doing that, I remember there was an old house we had out there, about five or six buildings; government funds built those little frame houses. I didn't claim it was mine, but the government people themselves said we are going to have to build you one. One day you can be old and not be able to work and not have money, but you will have a place to live. I said, "Okay, good." So it was done. That house happened to be there, and people were using it, different families, and they paid me. When we needed space there—I'm talking about where the community is, they call it a reservation now—we had that particular frame house. We needed space for the courthouse and offices, so I said there is a building out there that is supposed to belong to me, so let's move out there. We had started a little office here in town on Flagler Street. When we organized, we had to have an office, telephone, and everything, but we never had enough money to pay that rent. So we moved out there. I don't know how long it was the office, but they never paid me. Then we finished the other big building as an office; we moved in there, and that little house was empty again. We were looking around for a courthouse. We had a little jail, we had a police department, so we had to have the court. We didn't have a building; we don't have money for it. So I said, "Okay, go ahead and use it, but you have to pay me at least ten or fifteen dollars a month, something like that." I let them do it many times. I would never ask a penny, but the bookkeepers see this.

I had worked so hard, but never had a penny come from the tribe to me. They audited when we came out with a resolution on how much they were supposed to pay me weekly or by the month [as chairman]. They had never done it because they did not have that kind of money; they didn't have to pay me. The auditors said, "Mr. Tiger, you are supposed to be getting paid, but they never paid you. They owe you about six thousand dollars now. What are you going to do?"

I said, "They don't have money; one day when they have money, they should pay me, but right now they don't have it, so just say it is debt." They said, "Okay, that's what we are going to do. But that is for working [as chairman]."

The same way with my house, I didn't want to get paid because they didn't have money. The ten or fifteen dollars a month they were supposed to pay me, they will pay me. The court was there all right, so one day I thought, "Why should I charge them; why don't they just pay me and take over? I would take twenty-five thousand dollars, and they would just take over." So I told the councilmen and told everyone at the General Council meeting that's what I planned to do. So my sister, that family we were talking about, my own sister opposed it.

She said, "You want to sell that house?"

I said, "I'm not selling it. The tribe will just pay me and take over the house so I don't have to bother with it and they don't have to pay me anymore."

She said, "Well, you can't do that."

I said, "Well, maybe we can't, but I believe it can be done to get me off clean cut; just go ahead and pay it off." They didn't want to do that. I had to go on a long trip so I told Billy Cypress, "You go ahead and take care of that. I couldn't speak for myself anyhow. You are assistant chairman so take care of that. The tribe can pay me about fifteen thousand dollars; maybe they can pay me later." So the trip finished, and I got back, and Billy didn't talk to me so I talked to him: "How did you handle it?" [He said,] "Nobody listened to me. It was bad. Your own sister was trying to get you with that." So it was just one family, my sister and her youngsters, even though they are my own blood, turned against me on that, but I didn't care.

Elections are another thing; they didn't have to get involved in it. Those are the kinds of things I guess they used against me. I don't know; they never said that.

We had to vote on a bingo hall—accept it or oppose. And that happened at the 1985 election, too. We were going to spend that money to take care of the people, to take care of local issues. The people had agreed to that. The reason we said that was the BIA didn't have too much money, plus they were not giving enough money for health. Plus they were not giving us enough money for education or trying to help traditional language and all that learning—they were not paying for that. So I used that to convince my people to vote for bingo. That was a big issue, but I had never used it because some of those people [Tiger's opposition] wanted bingo money. They wanted to get in. That's why the individual we're talking about made a mess of my plan. He wanted to change; he made a mess, so that's why he lost [the office of chairman].

New Beginnings

I think maybe about over twenty years I stayed single; then I finally decided to get married, and we did, around 1985 or 1986. I got married to a young woman from Colombia. She's Spanish, but she seemed to be a fine young woman, and we both fell in love with each other.

She realized I was Indian, and I realized she was Spanish, but my mother talked to me about the Spanish years ago when I was younger. The Spanish people, Spanish women, they are pretty excitable, and sometimes they get pretty mean. Years ago when people married Spanish women, they used to get hurt sometimes. They really hurt you real bad. As far as our language, speaking our language and the Spanish-speaking people, it is not so far apart. You can always learn it fast enough—better than English. I always wondered why my mother said that to me. I thought I would go ahead and find out, and I took a chance and we got married. Her name is Yolima, and she speaks Spanish. She works with me in so many ways helping me, anything she can do with me. Or sometimes she does it because she wants to.

I'm busy these days. I have a little airboat operation out there in the Glades. She helps me drive the boats, and she helps run the gift shop. It's nice when someone can help you. We do that. I'm not in politics as much like I used to be, so I do a lot of the Miccosukee Indian crafts. I'm busy doing that, and she takes care of customers and speaks in both languages, English and Spanish. It helps me a lot. That's how we do it today, and that's what she does today.

Fig. 13. Buffalo Tiger's airboat ride business on the Tamiami Trail. Courtesy of Harry Kersey.

She told me before we got married that she had two young girls in Colombia. They were very small girls then. I told her she could go ahead and bring them here, and they can go to school here and learn English. One day that happened; the girls came here. They did not speak any English. They were small girls, and they were pretty cute girls. They are fine, nice girls. They started school and learned English fast. Now they can speak very good English and speak Spanish, too. Every year they have to go home to Colombia, and they learn more Spanish; then they come back and learn more English. One of them, Jennifer, is finishing high school. I don't know what she will be doing next; she might be going back to school later on. The younger one, Jessica, has not finished high school yet. I'm sure she will be going to university because she's a real good student. So that's what happened to this family.

I've gone to church, different types of churches, trying to find what other people believe. I have even gone to a Baptist church to see what they do. But what I learned in my life from my Breathmaker isn't taught in the churches. We learn in entirely different ways. But that always has been my heart and my life, so even though I believe what Christians like Baptists may say, I see it does not fit my life; but I do respect them. It seems to be a good way to feel. You believe in something; I believe in something.

Even today I talk to my wife often because she is Spanish and has different ways and expressions in her life. She is Catholic, and she respects my ways and I respect her ways. If I didn't do that, I probably wouldn't be here because I might be a drunkard, not believing in myself, and I would be doing wrong things.

But I do believe, and when I was learning, when I was younger, I learned pretty strong, and people respect that. It's something people tell you, and you just take it. You just grow up in it.

OUR HERITAGE, OUR LIFE, OUR FUTURE

Reclaiming Our Heritage

I think it's very important for us to establish what we're going to be calling Miccosukee Indian Village or Culture Center [on the Tamiami Trail]. But beyond that we should be thinking about it because it's very important to establish now, because in ten years or maybe forty to fifty years we are going to be looking back. And by that time things will be hard. We may be losing so many things. Not losing it, but forgetting about it when we don't practice that much like we did ten years ago, even today. So on that basis I believe we should establish a real traditional-practice life, what we call a village now. But if we do that, we might have to change it into something a little deeper than that.

What I see today, it's fine. Everybody's looking to make a buck to buy groceries or whatever they want to buy. That's why we are all working there.

But we must realize it is more than that. It's really something that is going to protect you, your culture, your customs, your language. You had things to do daily when you were living sixty years ago. We want to bring back that type of feeling. That is the place it will be. Really it's like a school for the Miccosukee students or other people interested in learning more about Miccosukees. They could learn there and be respectful; that's what it's all about. We need to be thinking in that way. We can get together and establish what we would like to see happen.

My thought is, I always felt we must keep traditional feelings, traditional practices, language, or culture. All that should be saved, be protected. Only way we could do that, we have to understand what's going to happen tomorrow. We have to realize more people are coming from other countries. Population is increasing in Dade County and Florida. It's heavy, and I don't know how long we are going to keep fighting and keep our land the way it is now.

One day we might find we don't have much of anything left. And maybe we all will speak English and forget about our language and traditional practice. But to have something and understand it well, you never lose that. That means you respect yourself and you have not forgotten yourself and keep learning. Even though you go to school and learn English, and you do things so you can make a buck to buy food, and we have to act like somebody else we call the white man—but knowing all the time we are brown people, or *Eelaponke*. But we can still work so many hours, so many days to make a little money to buy different things we need.

So that makes it hard for us. Once we start thinking about money, we forget about ourselves. Because all of us seem to want more money; if we can make more money doing this and doing that, you are going to go after that. And I don't blame you for feeling that. But if you train, you learn so strong and so well in your customs, your traditional practice and language, you will never forget. But you must practice almost every day. There should be a place for that for us. We might have to start developing material and use it there so we can learn more if we want to. And ask questions older people used to know pretty well—how traditional Indians, elder people, used to teach us, different things. Sooner or later, those elder people will be dying off, and then we have nothing. So we must quickly develop something there so we have something, at least so we don't forget ourselves who we are. So I will try to encourage us and myself to go ahead and do something with the Miccosukee Indian Village today. We might have to call it a different name.

I noticed we have gone pretty far away from what originally that village was meant to be. That's what money does to people. That's what all people—grandmothers, grandfathers, uncles, aunts—have taught us that's what will happen. That's what we are in today. But to have something to be proud of, we have to really understand what was the traditional Indian life Miccosukees were living at that time.

We did not have a television or radio or electric sewing machine. Our grandmothers used to use a needle and thread to make clothes for us. Our mothers learned from them. And they made clothes with old broken-down hand sewing machine. But the village should be representing that time. The way I see it, the village is hurting us if we don't take care of it like we are supposed to. We don't want to display television blasting away or radio, or electric sewing machines. I'm not scolding anybody, but we must recognize it's not what people used to do. And if a tourist comes and sees us, they are thinking we are faking them because we don't have any traditional life there—even though I know people working there are filled with feelings and understand who we are. But other people see us; they don't see it that way. They see we are too much influenced, too much taken away by white man's way and that's what we practice there. And also that we are not too concerned about it. And that is the way a lot of us see it. If we are going to live [the modern] way, we should not have to display it. We should do that back home.

So this camp must be changed to real traditional life for *Eelaponke*. It is easily done if we know how to do it. I believe some of us know what we need to do with that. It will take a little time and a little work. And people will have to practice it. But it is part of the job; that's what you are doing in your work there; it's very good. Should you add on more traditional ways, it doesn't mean we are trying to make you like people who lived sixty years ago. You cannot go back that far, we know that. We're not saying that. We just practice while we are there at the camp. You go home and change your attitude or feelings like you want it to be; you can do that. But there is a village, and if you want to do a good job and respect yourself and all traditional people, when you come to work you have to act like and do what they used to do. And what we are doing is not that way. We must ask the Miccosukee Indian school to bring children maybe thirty minutes or one hour so we can explain why it is that way. But we are not telling anybody to turn around and go back and live like sixty years ago. We are not telling people that. We must have one place for traditional practice, and that's what we have in the village. There is a different place for the yearly religious practice—the Green Corn Dance—but that is a different place we're talking about. It's strictly for us!

Respecting Our Life

Breathmaker tells Indians how to live, in very few words though. Not as many words as you people use in your Christian lives—very few, meaning so much. I hope you understand Indian people years ago had very few words on different things. We didn't have many words like other people have. Just too many words mean nothing now. You can see that. With us, we have very few words. If you say Breathmaker, it's a word. You know what that is. Breathmaker's word, it's everything.

Somebody might say, "Don't do that." That means if you are doing something wrong here, don't do it. Therefore we have to respect that. It's what we learned. Today a lot of those things are not used. That's what we need to start teaching our young people. Even though they go to school, they probably believe in something else, but they need to know what they have to respect.

We have to say to younger people, those are the kinds of things that are not written; you always have to learn from the elder people, and they will teach you. You have to ask to learn, and they'll be happy to teach you. That's what we have to do; you have to learn. I don't care what people say to me; I know what I know. That's the way my brothers and other people are. Those people not knowing anything, they can pick up a piece of paper and tell you this is the way it is. That's the way it is for you, but it's not the way it is for me.

We are talking about what Breathmaker created—those are the kinds of things I hope people would understand. Like we talk about this hurricane out there somewhere. Those are the kinds of things Breathmaker has made. It's a part of nature.

Everything is nature. We must learn that because it's life. It's not human like you and me, but even a tree is life. Those trees are going to die just like us, and those trees have a heart like us. They don't have blood but life. Everything's alive on this earth. It's Breathmaker's planet, and he has planted us here with the trees. Like it or not, that's the way we are. White-skinned people came from one island, red-skinned people came from another island, but we don't talk too much about white-skinned people because we only know ourselves what we learn from this earth.

Breathmaker talked to us after we were created. He told us, "I will return one day. Carry on what I have taught you to live by or otherwise I will destroy you." We were told before Breathmaker returns we will see signs like people changing to be disrespectful and people doing many wrong things. You will probably see more hurricanes, tornadoes, and earthquakes. You will probably see something you've never seen before on this earth because earth is getting hotter. You've never seen certain types of snakes around here before; they will probably be here. So many things will change, you see. We must keep that and believe that. So that's what our people know and always believe—something's going to happen someday soon, and they want to make sure we won't be something different.

When we were put on this earth, we were not even alive. He made us a life. We learned that Breathmaker is the one who made everything for us. The elders told us what to do and how to think. We are Breathmaker's people so we have to love nature and try to hang on to nature. Don't let nature die—that's what we are here for. Yes, it is something that must be understood and passed on.

Rekindling Our Future

This is how we live now. Many times we like to be close with others of our people. You can have a good feeling about each other and respect whoever you are working with. You want to help all you can and not hate but care. Do what you can for others, particularly your own family—your sons, daughters, your wife, your mother, and your father. It is fine to do that. In return your family will respect you. In other words, you have to care for each other like people say, like white man says, "We care and we love them." That is what we need.

It does not matter what happens, but we must keep learning in our life. We must learn our history, our culture, and other different things that are important. We can learn English, too, because we need it to work, but we should never forget who we are. We have a long way to go.

We don't know what will happen over the years, but we do know our Breathmaker has told us where we should go. We are trying to get there, so we must always learn from our parents, uncles, and grandmothers, who tell us what we are supposed to be doing and how to follow the direction where we are supposed to be going. A lot of times we forgot about those things, but we should talk to each other. You must do so. If you have a good friend or family member, talk with whomever you want about those things.

Never hate anybody, and never talk about anybody. Everybody has something good in them. We should understand and care for each other. Sometimes if you get to know a person, he or she could be a nice person. You should not just hurt or disrespect someone. We should help and care for each other because there are not too many Miccosukee people.

There are a lot of other things that are important. You must ask questions of your uncle, your grandmother, or grandfather. Sometimes your older brother even knows more culture talk, and you can ask to learn. Your mother knows culture talk, and you can ask her questions about it. If we do not ask questions about things, we stop learning and we are going to lose out. Miccosukee ways—culture, language, and all that—can be gone overnight. We do not want that to happen. We want people to speak our language. We want to keep the culture and traditional feeling of understanding. Those must keep going as long as we live. That is what we are here for, so we should be thinking about the culture. We must always remember what Breathmaker has given to us. We must keep it that way.

We do have a problem today with the people we call white man. We Miccosukee people have a place that is our Corn Dance ground. We had a place that was our Corn Dance ground for many years, and sometimes we change and move to other areas. Today we don't have much room to go different places as far as the Corn Dance ground is concerned. There is a problem that people in the white man's government want to control the area where we have our Corn Dance ground. This is something new and not something we started. Our Breathmaker tells us what to do with that problem, so we can only do what we think is best for us.

But today white men want to be in charge of the Corn Dance ground because the land situation is under the control of white men. We think we have a right to practice our spiritual beliefs. Our Breathmaker has given us what we have today. Our beliefs are strong, and we practiced our medicine this way for so many years without the white man, and we would like to keep it the way it always has been. We have a right to do so.

The problems we are facing are because of the water and land situation. We are not asking anybody to tell us what we can and cannot have. It has gone too far. We have practiced our religious beliefs without white men telling us what to do all these years. After white men discovered this country, we still practiced our beliefs. We strongly believe in our culture and should continue following our beliefs. The white man knows we have religious beliefs and we are following our beliefs, and they should leave us alone.

We are not bothering anybody, and in fact we go back in the woods so no one has to bother us. We always did that, and we should not change. We don't have to ask permission from the white man to have our Green Corn

Dance ground. The government of the United States must recognize that because their constitution points out that anyone has the right to practice their religious beliefs and should be protected. That is why we should continue and we don't have to be afraid of white men. We must make up our mind that we can continue our ways. We should do whatever we did before and practice that way.

Let's not bring in the white man's machines or concrete and things like that to try and make something different. That is the kind of thing they don't want us to do. As long as we don't bring in those things, nobody will tell us what to do. We are going to have to leave things alone, like bringing in heavy equipment or concrete. Pouring the concrete makes it look like white man's work, and that should not be done. That is not the way our Breathmaker has told us to do. We are just making it harder for ourselves so white men can try to take our beliefs away from us. We don't want that to happen.

We should discuss this. We must believe strongly that we should keep our Green Corn Dance land, not only just in one area for one group but for *Cheeshaponke* near Lake Okeechobee and Big Cypress and all *Eelaponke* down here. It should be kept for those people who have practiced it over the years for years and years past. We have kept our beliefs and look after ourselves and what little we have left.

Miccosukee people should wear something that identifies their own customs. The way we dress is part of our culture, too. Years ago Miccosukees wore their own clothing. Today we are at a point where we are all wearing other people's clothing. Very few people still wear traditional clothes. It is vital that we realize how far away we have drifted from using our customary clothes. We must stop and examine why little boys, little girls, women, or men are not wearing their customary clothing. The reasons could be because it's easier to buy different types of clothes than it is to make hand-sewn clothes. Also, when it gets old or worn out, it can be thrown away and easily replaced. Another reason is the cost to make Miccosukee clothes is rather expensive, making it difficult for many to buy them or to make them. The clothes people wear today are made of cotton fabric and other manmade materials. Miccosukee people wore buckskin clothing and clothing made from palmetto fiber before the introduction of cotton fabric. We changed our style of clothing and the material used to make it as we adapted to more modern times. It is important to recognize the people still wearing their customary clothing.

When we talk about healthy food in the Miccosukee way, we are talking about different things. Our people like to hunt for their food. There are many things the people can hunt. They have to know the types of animals that live in this area now that they can or cannot eat. Miccosukees should talk about the types of birds they can or cannot eat. We eat plenty of birds. While there are birds we can eat, there are many birds that we cannot eat. We lived on fish years ago. There were plenty in the Glades, even in the salt water. We have to know what types of fish we can eat and those we cannot eat. Our bodies were used to eating fish and turtles. We have to know the different kinds of turtles we can eat. Our bodies are used to food we grew up eating.

We also now have sickness from food. Our bodies are not completely accepting the white man's food. Non-Indian doctors and Miccosukee doctors acknowledge that we are now all sick. We realize that this is the truth. Miccosukees need to come together, the different clans should gather, to discuss these problems and determine a solution. Recently, we changed the food we eat. We eat beef, hamburgers and hot dogs, cold drinks, ice cream, cakes, and breads. Those kinds of food are easy to get if you have the money, and that is changing the types of foods our bodies are used to. We are healthy in many ways, but our bodies are not healthy now. Our Indian people used to be big and tall but not heavy. Indians are short and heavy today. We have heart problems, high blood pressure, kidney problems, high cholesterol, and diabetes from too much sugar. There are many things wrong with our people today. Maybe we are changing the types of food we eat too quickly. Maybe we should start adding new foods to our diet slowly, until our bodies get used to them.

It is easy for Miccosukees to get into trouble with drinking problems, or become alcoholics, as people with those problems are called. Indian people seem to have had *keehoome* for a long time, but never as much as they do now. They knew not to overdo it. Today we do not think about what is going to happen tomorrow. We just go ahead and have fun and drink all we can until we are drunk. It makes us sick because alcohol is very hot and burns our insides. It will damage our bodies. Some parts of the inside of the body are delicate and burn when alcohol gets to them. We should think about trying to take care of our bodies and ourselves better. We should look at our families and ourselves. We should think about all of our people.

As for Everglades' water, everything has changed. The water was very clean years ago. Miccosukees would swim in the Glades water and drink it. Today people are saying that the water is not clean. You can tell that is true because it is yellow-looking and does not look like water you would want to drink. You would probably get sick from drinking it. That means that fish or alligators in the water are not healthy; white men did that, not Indians. Miccosukees were told that was what was going to happen many years ago, and now it has. We cannot just say that the water is no good or the land is no good and turn our back on that.

In years back, elders were always telling us what type of things we used to do. If we are not doing what we are supposed to do, we will lose it. We will lose it, and we will be sorry later. We have lost the Snake Dance, as people used to call it. Not too long ago we went to Snake Dance. Now we don't even have them. I don't know how it happened, but it slipped through our hands. I don't believe we could get that back because most of us don't know how that works. These are the kind of things I am talking about. We can lose the Green Corn Dance easily. We can lose our language easily.

We can be lost ourselves.

I'm sure I know that most of the Miccosukee people don't want that to happen. You don't want to be lost with other people, too many other people.

To Miccosukee councilmen: I know how councilmen feel when you work on something and you need help. You have no one to talk to; you stand alone. You need understanding, but people do not understand you. It's a hard job you do, much like this book has been hard for me.

AFTERWORD

The Importance of a Life

Harry A. Kersey Jr.

Among the Plains Indian cultures of the nineteenth century great emphasis was placed on experiencing a "vision quest," in which an adult male established direct communication with the supernatural spirits that would
direct his life. It could take place at the time of rites of passage, during the
Sun Dance ceremony, or at virtually any point an individual was willing to
undergo the mental preparation and physical deprivation required to in-
duce such an experience.[1] It was usually preceded by a time of prayer and
fasting in which the mind was cleared and made receptive to the coming of
spiritual beings. If all went well, an Indian man communed with his
guardian spirits, receiving instruction in those things that would guide
him through life.[2] He learned the sacred items he would carry in his medicine bundle to ward off evil and bring success in the hunt and warfare.
These items made up a highly personal collection with meaning only for
the individual, unlike the larger communal medicine bundle or other
sacred items that held a corporate meaning for the tribe as a whole. From
the spirits an individual also learned his war song and death song, which
spelled out his prowess and the expressed importance of his life.[3] Although southeastern Indians did not institutionalize the vision quest to
such a degree, there were certainly beliefs in individual spirit bundles that
protected one in battle, as well as medicine bundles that contained the
sacred ritual items of the group.[4] Among the Florida Indian tribes the latter
were handled exclusively by medicine men at the time of the Green Corn
Dance.[5] By this century the Miccosukees had left many of the old traditions
behind, and most young men did not have war songs or medicine songs.
Therefore Buffalo Tiger's narrative stands as a statement of the principles
and beliefs that guided his life and that of his people.

[127]

Buffalo Tiger's life history is an important document in both the cultural and the political domains. First, it is a tribal elder's personalized and detailed retrospective on Miccosukee culture and beliefs in the twentieth century. It expands our understanding of a people undergoing rapid and fundamental cultural transition, and it allows a comparison with accounts of the same period provided by non-Indians, many of whom worked with tribal informants. Second, the story is an insider's view of Indian survival politics at the national level from the 1950s through the 1980s. Tiger provides many missing elements in the chronicle of why the Miccosukee tribe was recognized despite the national trend toward termination, and he reveals how a small, obscure tribe secured reservation lands and ultimately achieved economic stability. In this unique collaborative autobiography Buffalo Tiger emerges as one of the truly significant figures in the Indian self-determination movement.

Miccosukee Culture

It is now well understood that the cosmology of southeastern Indians posited a world in which reality was constantly being pulled in opposite directions by contrary powers. The spiritual beings of the Upper World and the Lower World were always in contention, and the residents of This World sought to maintain equilibrium.[6] Only the "Maker of Breath," whom the Muskogees called *Hesakadum Esee* (in Hitchiti, *Feshahkee-ommehche*), the giver and taker of life, kept things in balance. The Maker of Breath had communicated customs, medicines, and principles to the people that enabled them to live their lives in the best order possible. He was the maker of all things in life: pure water, abundant corn, and the successful hunt. He was the god esteemed above all other spiritual beings.[7] These general descriptions of Breathmaker's powers as perceived by the Creeks, Seminoles, Choctaws, and other southeastern tribes do not address the specific ways this deity affects Indian life.

The small number of systematic studies on Miccosukee beliefs and rituals tell us little about Breathmaker. In the 1940s and 1950s Louis Capron of West Palm Beach, a long-time friend of the Muskogee-speaking Cow Creek Seminoles who lived north of Lake Okeechobee, frequently attended their Green Corn Dance.[8] Although not a trained ethnologist, he was the first to provide a detailed description of the Seminole/Miccosukee busk ceremony and to emphasize the central role of the medicine bundle. According to his study there was originally only one medicine bundle, the contents of which and their uses were received in mythological times from the culture hero.[9] The two original medicine men, one from the Tiger clan and one from the Wind clan, were instructed in the use of the medicines by an individual identified as the adopted son of the Corn Mother. When changing conditions make a new medicine necessary, the supreme being causes it to appear in the medicine bundle during the last night of the busk; the medicine man discovers it there the next morning when wrapping the individual items for storage. Conversely, a bad medicine man, one who does not serve his people well, can cause medicine to disappear from the bundle.[10] During the Seminole wars much of the medicine was lost or went west with groups of captives, since small bundles of medicine were made up from the main one for the use of individual war parties. At the end of the Seminole wars three bundles were left in Florida.[11] These bundles and the medicine men who owned them were the basis for three ceremonial groups, each holding an annual busk and following its council of elders.

The anthropologist William C. Sturtevant studied and wrote about the Miccosukees of Florida, primarily in the 1950s. In his classic work "Medicine Bundles and Busks of the Florida Seminole," based on fieldwork among the Miccosukees of the Tamiami Trail, Sturtevant concluded that the medicine bundles played no role in the busk ceremony of the old Creek towns.[12] Moreover, his main informant, himself a former medicine man, did not attribute much importance to supernatural beings in bringing the medicine: he "laid more emphasis on the role of the two original medicine men in the discovery of the medicine. Some specific items are also, traditionally, gifts of various supernatural beings, chiefly the Thunders and associated supernaturals."[13] It is noteworthy that neither Capron nor Sturtevant emphasized the name *Breathmaker* in their accounts, perhaps because their informants did not use the term. Both writers focused on describing the medicine bundles and their function in relation to the busk ceremony.

The medicine bundles were recognized as the symbols and powers around which Seminole ceremonial and political life revolved and were believed necessary for existence of the group. The medicines were seen as capable of doing great harm or of losing potency, so it was important that they be protected from harmful influences. Thus Sturtevant noted, "These beliefs make it exceedingly difficult to obtain detailed or reliable information on the esoteric aspects of Seminole religion, and the normal inarticulateness with outsiders, due in part to inadequate control of English but even more suspicion of the motives of the questioner, make it wellnigh impossible to explore thoroughly the ramifications, interrelations, and significance of Seminole religious beliefs and practices."[14]

Sturtevant's later works provide extensive biographical information on two significant Miccosukee elders. In "A Seminole Medicine Maker" the anthropologist described and analyzed an ambivalent relationship with his primary informant, the former medicine man Josie Billie.[15] By that time Josie had adopted Christianity and revealed little about his former beliefs; he said more about the ingredients and curative powers of native medicine than about the source of its power. The life story of Sam Huff as related to Sturtevant is the subject of "A Seminole Personal Document."[16] Neither of these informants provided significant information about Miccosukee/ Seminole perceptions of an intimate relationship with a supreme being. A 1970 article on Josie Billie by Miami physician William M. Straight reported, "It now became his duty to accompany the medicine man at dawn on the fourth day of the Green Corn Dance as he bathed ceremonially, and chanted songs to the Great Being (Fee-sa kee-kee o-meek-chee in Miccosukee; Sa-kee tom-mas-see in Cow Creek), asking personal protection as they handled the powerful medicine in the medicine bundle, and finally to go into the woods and return with the medicine bundle."[17] Nevertheless, it was not until the writings of Charles M. Hudson, Joel W. Martin, and others that the centrality of the Maker of Breath in Creek cosmology—and by extension that of the Miccosukees and Seminoles as well—became widely known.

Buffalo Tiger provides an intimate account of a traditional Indian's relationship to Breathmaker. He tells us that early in this century his people still believed that Breathmaker created the land, the water, and life itself. They celebrated the Green Corn Dance in part to honor his beneficence, as well as to bind the people together in a reaffirmation of their religious beliefs and social values. Breathmaker provided the medicine bundle's sacred items, which were viewed once a year during the busk ceremony. Medicine men studied many years to learn the meaning and use of the medicine; youngsters with the gift to become spiritual leaders were often identified early and groomed for that role.

Individual Indians believed in a panoply of gods and spirits, but they acknowledged Breathmaker as all-powerful and prayed in his name. He had created Indian people out of the brown mud—thus accounting for their skin color—and allowed them to come forth from the bowels of the earth. Moreover, he divided the people into clans named for animals or natural phenomena and gave each clan a special function in facilitating the life of the people. As in most southeastern tribes, Miccosukee kinship is matrilineal. Strict rules governed the relationships between the clans, such as the role each played during the busk ritual: Panther and Wind clans provided medicine men, the Big City clan served as "lawyers" during the court sessions, and Birds controlled the dance ground precinct. The strictest rules were those prohibiting marriage within one's own clan or with individuals from closely linked clans. Some clans served as "big brothers" to other clans, and the rules of exogamy applied equally in such instances.

Buffalo Tiger's narrative offers insight into some little-explored aspects of Miccosukee beliefs concerning religious symbolism, such as the four compass directions and the colors associated with them. The medicine men always face east when preparing sacred medicines. East, where the sun rises and everything begins, is represented by the color white. By contrast, west is associated with death and evil and is always depicted by the color black. The directions north and south are more value neutral. A Miccosukee can sleep with his head pointed in any direction but west, but at death the body is laid in a shallow grave with the head pointing west—the direction in which the departing spirit moves. A change in Miccosukee mortuary practices noted by Buffalo Tiger—above-ground burial—reflected a need to release the deceased's spirit as quickly as possible.

Throughout his account Buffalo Tiger emphasizes the importance of venerating elders. They were always to be respected and consulted by the young people. He also speaks respectfully of the *ouwayachee*—ancient ones who were in Florida before his people arrived. It was the grandparents who had fought to keep the land and preserve the Miccosukee way of life. They had learned the laws Breathmaker made and passed them along. Now young people must learn these laws in order to know who they are. If white laws are substituted for Indian laws, if foreign ways are adopted to the exclusion of Indian ways, the Miccosukees will no longer continue to exist as a people. Someday Breathmaker will return to see how the Miccosukees are doing, to see that they have preserved the laws and nature as he prescribed. Meanwhile, the Indians know he is out there through the hurricane and other natural phenomena. Buffalo Tiger believes that when Breathmaker returns, the Indians must know who they are and show that they live according to Breathmaker's laws.

Perhaps the most poignant portraits of a disappearing culture are found in Buffalo Tiger's vivid recollections of everyday life in the Miccosukee camp. His earliest memories are of his grandparents, especially *Posi*— Grandmother. Although his grandfather operated a store and made money trading with other Indians, everyone acknowledged his grandmother as the camp matriarch. She was a Bird clan member, as were all the adult women in the family and their children. They taught youngsters such as Mostaki what it meant to be a member of the Bird clan and what was expected of them by way of good behavior. Occasionally, children who disobeyed or caused trouble were scratched on the arm with needles that drew blood although there were times when adults simply threw water on them. A Miccosukee child learned to make do with a few simple playthings— hand-carved toys, a bow and arrow, some penned animals for pets. However, the entire Everglades was his playground. Traveling by canoe from camp to camp with his family introduced an Indian youngster to the intricacies of navigating through the trackless sawgrass. Hunting, fishing, and swimming with his brothers and cousins occupied much of young Buffalo Tiger's time. He spent hours observing the feeding habits and movements of fish, turtles, and birds, developing the observational skills he would need to become a successful hunter. Whenever a young boy observed a bird or animal he would describe it to his elders and they would explain what it was and whether it was edible or not. Later, when a boy was older he would accompany the men on their hunting expeditions, scouting out the game, taking his dog along on the hunt, assisting in the kill, and learning how to keep the canoes and other equipment.

One of Buffalo Tiger's most gripping tales tells how his family survived the great hurricane of 1926 that devastated southern Florida. He and his family were in transit across the Everglades when the storm struck; they survived by finding a high hammock—which had to be shared with snakes and other animals. The small children were covered with a tarpaulin and lashed to a large tree throughout the storm. They stayed warm only by passing around the youngest child and clasping him a few minutes at a time to absorb body heat. When the storm passed, the Indians retrieved their canoes and continued the journey back to their camp only to find it destroyed. This story is one of the few detailed accounts of Indian survival of the 1926 disaster.

Another venue where the Miccosukee child learned from his elders was in the sleeping *chickee* at night. Indian families ate and slept together on plank platforms erected under a thatched-roof shelter. After they had washed for the evening and dropped the mosquito netting, young children snuggled down and watched the stars while family members told them folk tales that conveyed the values of their people. One of the first things they learned was not to run about at night outside the friendly confines of the campfire; darkness was the domain of spirits, and the living moved about only during daylight hours. If clothes were washed and hung out to dry, they were always taken in before nightfall or evil spirits might penetrate them. Children were also taught never to harm small creatures such as spiders and bugs; they were told that if you gratuitously destroy those smaller than yourself, something large might come and destroy you!

When a boy reached the age of fifteen or so, he was ready to receive his adult name. The boy's parents usually selected the name of an Indian man who was already deceased and whose memory they wished to honor. This name was suggested to the Miccosukee council of elders for consideration, for it was the council that actually bestowed the name at the time of the Green Corn Dance. During the day preceding the naming ceremony boys went without food or sleep but engaged in the dancing and other activities. If they went to sleep, their naming was postponed until the following year. When the time came for Buffalo Tiger to receive his man's name, Heenehatche, his father accompanied him to the council meeting. The councilmen questioned him about his lineage and clan and the meaning of his name. Again, this story is one of the most complete accounts of how an individual received his adult name. Of course, it had nothing to do with the anglicized name William Buffalo Tiger, bestowed on him in later years by non-Indians. The first part, Buffalo, was a nickname based on his loping stride while playing sports, and the second came from his father's name, Tiger Tiger. While working in an aircraft factory during World War II, the young Indian received the given name William from a plant foreman who was dissatisfied with the name Buffalo Tiger. This account is yet another twist in the strange ethnocentric saga of how Indians acquired their English surnames.

Indian people learned to make medicine from plants to treat children and adults, and the materials were often difficult to collect. Moreover, the cures were occasionally as much spiritual as physical. Buffalo Tiger provides a personal account of having been cured from an affliction induced by a dream about spiders. He had not contacted or been bitten by a real spider, but the dream led to his paralysis and near death. A medicine woman correctly interpreted the cause of his ailment and mixed the medicine that cured him. His brother had a similar experience after dreaming about a monkey. This account confirmed that much of Miccosukee medicine revolved around finding the correct source of illness—was it physical or spiritual? Many Miccosukees knew how to prepare medicines from leaves, barks, and mosses, but only experienced medicine men and women could divine the spiritual causes of illnesses. It took many years of study to learn how to make the medicines and use them correctly. This was a gift with mixed blessings, however, because a person who was in touch with the spiritual world could be accused of using that power negatively to engage in witchcraft. To ward off their enemies, medicine men actively cultivated the belief that they dabbled in the occult, but medicine women were especially vulnerable to such accusations.

The day-to-day rhythms of the Miccosukee camp taught both boys and girls what would be expected of them. Boys learned how to participate in the dancing at the Green Corn ceremony. When they reached their late teens, they were taken under the direct tutelage of their uncles—their clan fathers. Buffalo Tiger remembers that by the time a boy was that age he was eligible to take a wife and start his own family. The families and clan elders normally arranged marriages. The girls learned from their mothers and aunts the domestic skills necessary to keep a home. Corn was the staple food of the Miccosukees. The grain was placed in a mortar made from a log and then pounded into meal with a huge wooden pestle. This task took strength and patience. Miccosukees used the same process in the last century to make coontie (flour) from the wild Zamia root. Corn was also boiled and roasted, but mostly it was used to make the thick liquid food known as sofkee. The corn gruel was brought to a boil then left to simmer. Every camp had a pot of sofkee available throughout the day, and since there was no set mealtime, Indians and visitors were free to eat at their leisure. If families ate a meal together, it was usually coincidental.

Miccosukee women became expert seamstresses using small, lightweight Singer and White sewing machines purchased from traders in Miami, Fort Lauderdale, or Fort Myers. These hand-cranked models were ideal for use while the women sat on the platforms of the chickees. Initially, the family clothing, made from cloth purchased with cash earned from hunting, was relatively plain. Early in this century, however, Miccosukee and Seminole women began making the elaborate and colorful patchwork for which they are now noted. The patchwork not only decorated the clothing of family members but also became a popular item for sale to the tourists who flocked to south Florida during the winter. As a child Buffalo Tiger wore the traditional "great shirt" that hung to his knees, with just a bit of patchwork at the neck; he always went barefoot. The men of his camp wore an adult version of the "great shirt" and went barefoot; the women were beginning to wear skirts covered with elaborate bands of patchwork. By the time he was a young man, many Miccosukee males had begun to adopt a combination of store-bought trousers and shirts made from strips of Indian patchwork. This outfit was often worn with boots and topped with a cowboy hat. It was not uncommon to see such garb on the streets of Miami in the late 1930s and early 1940s.

Completion of the Tamiami Trail across the Everglades in 1928 brought several immediate changes to Miccosukee life. The heyday of hunting and trapping for a living was coming to an end. A few Indian men had worked on the road crews, and for most it was their first entry into wage labor. Now they also had more immediate access to Miami, either by driving over the road in old Model T trucks or by poling their canoes in the adjacent canals. Some Indians relocated their camps to the roadside and opened "native villages" that attracted tourists to view their families and a few penned animals. The Indian agent James L. Glenn constantly railed against "this professional freakism," as he put it, as well as the exploitation of Indian families who lived part of the year in the white-owned tourist villages of Miami.[18] His goal was to establish large rural Indian reservations in Florida, but he overlooked the fact that Miccosukees had long resisted government intervention in their lives. They preferred their Everglades camps and were adapting at their own pace to the tourist-oriented south Florida economy.

The opportunity to live in the commercial tourist villages of Miami, such as Coppinger's Tropical Gardens and Musa Isle, became a cultural transitional experience for a great many Miccosukee Indians.[19] That was certainly the case for Buffalo Tiger and his family, who found it congenial to spend several months each year in one of these settings. There they were paid to carry on the essential daily camp functions performed in the Everglades, only in this case with a tourist audience. Moreover, it provided an opportunity for the Indians to sell their handicrafts to northern visitors. To the extent that they were free to come or go as they pleased, the Miccosukees found it a convenient place in which to spend part of their time and supplement their income. It is noteworthy that Buffalo Tiger's uncle, Willie Willie, was the first entrepreneur to establish an "Indian village" in Miami in the 1920s, and he became well known to personages such as Al Capone. Before that time Indians had been employed to wrestle alligators or sell crafts at other tourist attractions, but there was no full-scale village until Willie Willie opened his at Musa Isle. After losing control of the Musa Isle location under mysterious circumstances, Willie Willie opened another commercial village in Hialeah, only to have it destroyed by the 1926 hurricane. At that point he retired to the Dania Indian reservation; however, he never ceased urging his family to let young Buffalo Tiger attend school. He correctly foresaw that the Indians could not continue to live traditional lives in the Everglades or work in amusement parks; they would need an education. Nevertheless, the family refused to let Buffalo or his siblings attend school, either in Miami or at the Dania (later named Hollywood) reservation day school that opened in 1927.[20]

Tiger's decision to marry a non-Indian woman, start a family, and live in suburban Miami away from his people had several consequences. Initially, there was some alienation from the Indian community and suspicion that he had become "too white." The racially mixed couple worked to show that they were committed to serving the Indian people, however, and gradually they overcame resistance to the marriage. Tiger's wife assisted as a midwife and took an active role in the political meetings leading up to federal recognition of the Miccosukee Tribe. She often talked of becoming a lawyer to help the Indian people. Eventually, she was accepted to the extent that the medicine men openly discussed conducting induction ceremonies that would lead to her becoming "spiritually Indian." Even so, for many years Buffalo Tiger was limited in the degree to which he could participate in the Green Corn Dance. When Buffalo's wife finished her education at the University of Miami, their two worlds grew apart. Although his first marriage ended in divorce, Buffalo's two sons are active members of the Miccosukee Tribe. A second marriage, also to a non-Indian woman, was similar in tone. His new wife came from a rural background and was also well accepted by the Miccosukees. She and Buffalo served as interpreters for elderly Indians when they came into town for shopping or medical care. That union also ended in divorce, but their three children all graduated from college and remain proud of their Indian heritage.

Throughout this difficult period of his life, when work was scarce and he had a family to raise, Buffalo Tiger was honing his English and acquiring knowledge of the outside world. During the war years he attended adult vocational school for several months to improve his language skills. Other than his cousin Mike Osceola, who graduated from high school in Miami and worked as an airline mechanic, Buffalo Tiger was the individual best qualified to speak for the Miccosukee people when they began their struggle for federal recognition in the 1950s. Still, the Miccosukee medicine men and council took their time in making the selection. They apparently wanted to observe how he conducted his affairs and formulate some opinion about his non-Indian wife. Finally, after a year had passed, the old medicine man Ingraham Billie and the council informed Buffalo Tiger that he would be their spokesman. In this position, which had no power or prestige, he would convey their ideas, not his own, to the state and federal governments. Nevertheless, their clear message was that with experience and maturity Buffalo Tiger would become a leader of the Miccosukee people. His first assignment was to work with his friend Robert Mitchell of Orlando, head of the Seminole Indian Association, in an effort to have state officials prevent game wardens from harassing Miccosukee camps by asking to see what the Indians had been hunting and fishing in the Everglades.

Miccosukee Government

The 1950s were a period of turmoil and political danger for American Indian tribes. The Republican-dominated Congress that came to power in 1946 set out to cut government expenses after the excessive spending of the New Deal and World War II. Conservative congressional leaders, especially those from the western states, were interested in eliminating Indian reservations and ending the government-to-government relationship that existed with the tribes. They called for closing the Bureau of Indian Affairs, terminating services to tribes, and assimilating Indians into the mainstream of American life.[21] To achieve these goals, they needed the support of Democrats, many of whom became convinced that the BIA was a paternalistic agency preventing Indians from exercising their civil rights and that reservations were anachronistic relics. Accordingly, in 1953 Congress passed House Concurrent Resolution 108, which spelled out the so-called termination policy, although the word *termination* was never mentioned and the document was couched in the rhetoric of freedom and civil rights for Indians.[22] The act identified specific tribes for termination of government services and sale of their reservation lands. Later in the same session Congress also passed PL-280, transferring civil and criminal jurisdiction over Indian crimes to the states. Ultimately, twelve states took advantage of this law.

The Seminoles of Florida—which subsumed the Miccosukees—were one of the tribes marked for elimination. Seminole termination bills were introduced in both houses of Congress, and hearings were scheduled before a joint session of the House and Senate Subcommittees on Indian Affairs. The first hearing was convened in Washington on 1–2 March 1953, and a large delegation of Florida Indians was present to give testimony.[23] Numerous non-Indian civic and political leaders, plus a leading anthropologist from the Smithsonian Institution, also testified against the bills. No effective national Indian organizations existed at that time to actively oppose the termination process. The National Council on Indian Affairs had been organized in 1944 but was still ineffectual, so each tribe was essentially on its own. It was during the Washington session, and at subsequent hearings held in Florida the following year, that Buffalo Tiger moved the Miccosukees into the forefront of Indian survival politics.

Senator Arthur Watkins of Utah, the most ardent supporter of termination, chaired the Washington hearings. Representative James Haley of Sarasota, a supporter of the Seminoles, and Senator George Smathers of Miami, who had attended high school with Miccosukees, represented Florida on the subcommittees. Buffalo Tiger and attorney Morton Silver spoke for the Miccosukees. When their term came to testify, Silver immediately alienated many of the legislators and others present with his abrasive presentation claiming that the Miccosukees owned most of Florida and thus were the legitimate representatives of all Florida Indians, including the great majority that lived on federal reservations. These claims were based on some questionable assumptions and the unratified "Macomb Treaty" from 1839. Buffalo Tiger was far less confrontational. With his calm demeanor and low-key rhetorical style, he quickly gained the attention of the congressmen. He engaged in a protracted exchange with Senator Smathers that clearly showed how opposed the Miccosukees were to any government intervention. When asked if his people would consider sending their children to school, Tiger replied that Miccosukees were upset over the bill because they thought it would change their law and way of life: "It is too involved for the Indians. I think they would be unhappy to do it right away."[24]

The Seminoles who lived on reservations strongly opposed termination and requested that government services and protection of their lands be extended for twenty-five more years.[25] Only Mike Osceola, a well-educated Indian representing a small number of Tamiami Trail families, spoke in favor of the termination plan. Then Senator Smathers sought to identify conditions under which the Miccosukees might accept termination. He asked if they would object if the government assured them that their land could not be stolen, if their land was placed in an Indian corporation to be used for the general benefit of all their people. When Tiger still demurred, Smathers asked, "You say we should do nothing. Is that what you are saying, to leave everything as it is?" Tiger replied calmly, "It would be easier for you, I imagine."[26] Smathers never convinced Buffalo Tiger that the bill could protect his people by vesting title to the land in the Indians themselves. Watkins, too, pursued the theme that Indians would have ownership of the land, something that their children could inherit. This approach totally missed the point that the Indians believed they already had a right to the land through treaties and prior usage; they had no interest in the concept of property in severalty. "I will tell you now," Tiger replied, "I am pretty sure my people won't like that. . . . This bill you are speaking about now is just a bad thing."[27] The confusing and often contradictory testimony underscored the friction that existed between the on- and off-reservation Indians as well as a split among the Miccosukees themselves. At the end of two days of hearings Senator Smathers declared, "Mr. Chairman, I do not know where we are. I came up here to find out what was going on, and we succeeded in getting me even more confused about this bill."[28] Most subcommittee members shared this confusion about how to proceed on Seminole (and Miccosukee) termination, and as a result no further action was taken on the bills for the remainder of the year.

While the hearings were in session, a dramatic confrontation took place on the Capitol steps. A Miccosukee delegation presented their so-called Buckskin Declaration (the message was inscribed on deerskin decorated with egret plumes) to a representative of President Eisenhower. In this document the Miccosukee General Council set forth a brief history of relations between the Florida Indians and the United States since 1821 and attacked the land claim that the reservation Seminoles had filed in 1950 seeking monetary compensation for past injustices. The Miccosukees disavowed any interest in payment for the Florida land and held that the claim was against their best interests. The document expressed their desire to continue a traditional lifestyle free of government interference. Finally, they declared they wished to deal directly with a representative of the president rather than the BIA. This political grandstanding incensed many of the congressmen and government officials, who suspected that attorney Morton Silver—whom many believed had Communist sympathies—had orchestrated it. That suspicion was confirmed when Silver and Buffalo Tiger deluged the White House with letters and telegrams demanding recognition that their group spoke for all Florida Indians. President Eisenhower rebuffed these overtures and urged them to operate through official channels. Nevertheless, the president notified the Miccosukees that the commissioner of Indian affairs would come to Florida to assess the situation.

In the fall of 1954 Commissioner Glenn Emmons went to Florida and met with all major Indian groups. Emmons's first meeting with Miccosukee leaders was held at Jimmy Tiger's camp on the Tamiami Trail with at least a dozen reporters and photographers from news agencies in attendance. The following day the BIA officials and Indians met at Silver's office in Miami. As a result of these meetings Commissioner Emmons gained a clear understanding of the Florida situation. He reported that the Miccosukee General Council was a legitimate group representing some 375 Indians—at best a bare majority of the Miccosukee-speaking population. He dismissed the claim that there were separate Miccosukee and Muskogee/Seminole nations, finding their cultures to be virtually identical. The most meaningful cleavage existing among Florida Indians was not between Miccosukees and Muskogees but between a mixed group of Miccosukees and Muskogees residing on three federal reservations and a predominantly Miccosukee off-reservation population. The reservation Indians generally accepted the framework of the non-Indian society around them and wanted to improve their social and economic status. By contrast, the Miccosukees—often called "Trail Indians"—deliberately rejected non-Indian society and preferred to maintain their traditional subsistence-level hunting and fishing economy. Furthermore, these broad categories were not definitive; the lines were so fluid that there were probably families in each group that, if forced, would join the other.

The question of federal recognition for the Miccosukees became a contentious issue. Silver claimed that the Miccosukees had a right to some five million acres of southern Florida through the 1839 "Macomb Treaty." They did not want the usual legal title to land, only the recognition of their rights to perpetual and exclusive use. They also demanded the prevention of further incursions on their land and federal recognition of the Miccosukee General Council. Emmons attempted to establish a common basis for understanding. He emphasized the desirability of dividing Florida Indians into two broad groups with a referendum or plebiscite allowing each adult Indian to choose which one to join. This opportunity would be available to each Indian youngster until the age of twenty-one. Emmons then sketched a plan for setting aside several thousand acres of Everglades land for the Trail Indians. Buffalo Tiger and Silver agreed and began marking areas on a map that the commissioner could take back to Washington. The land they designated included much of the Florida State Indian Reservation established in 1917, part of which was being used by Seminole cattlemen. Moreover, Emmons realized it would not be an easy task to resolve the Miccosukee claims for land and recognition, given the current national political climate so hostile to creating new tribes.

When the Eighty-fourth Congress convened in January 1955, the sentiment for termination remained strong, and there was a possibility that the Seminole termination bill would be reintroduced. The House Subcommittee on Indian Affairs, now chaired by Congressman Haley, scheduled additional hearings to be held in Florida. The first of these information-gathering sessions, held in Clewiston on 5 April 1955, saw a parade of witnesses who preponderantly opposed Seminole termination.[29] At the end of the meeting Haley indicated his own reluctance to end federal services to the Seminole people in the near future. The following day the subcommittee reconvened at Jimmie Tiger's camp on the Tamiami Trail. Again, Morton Silver and his associates enraged the congressmen with their claim that Miccosukees could speak for all Indians in Florida, the demand for immediate recognition, and threats of taking their case to international tribunals such as the United Nations and World Court. Buffalo Tiger took exception to Silver's extreme position that the General Council should speak for all Indians in Florida. He again made it clear that the Miccosukees were not a party to the Seminoles' $50 million claim pending before the Indian Claims Commission. "We don't want a claim for money," he stated, "we want a claim for land."[30] By the end of the Florida hearings the committee was apparently content to let the issue of Seminole termination die. In April 1955 Haley wrote to the head of the Seminole Indian Association, a major opponent of termination, stating, "I have not reintroduced the same bill that I introduced last year for the Seminoles . . . I sincerely do not think that the passage of such a bill at the present time would be beneficial to the Seminole Tribe."[31] As Senator Smathers succinctly put it some years later, "We killed the bill."[32]

It may be questioned why the Florida Indians, impoverished, poorly educated, and greatly in need of government services for survival, were ever considered for termination. One analysis focuses on the role of Congressman James Haley, especially after he assumed the chairmanship of the House Indian Affairs Subcommittee. Haley, a Democrat, was a fiscal conservative who generally supported Indian termination, and he apparently believed that the Indians from his own state should be subjected to the same scrutiny as other tribes. He was well aware of the Seminole/Miccosukee situation and evidently counted on the subcommittee hearings to reveal that they were not ready for termination—which is precisely what happened.[33] In retrospect, the Florida Indians were most fortunate that Smathers and Haley held positions on their respective subcommittees and could safeguard tribal interests throughout the termination period. As a rule those subcommittees were dominated by westerners who supported an anti–Indian rights agenda. One unintended outcome of these hearings was Buffalo Tiger's emergence as a respected voice for the Miccosukees. Tribal elders may have considered him merely their spokesman, but to officials in Washington and Tallahassee he had become the Miccosukee leader.

Having successfully avoided termination, the Seminoles moved quickly to protect themselves by organizing a tribal government under provisions of the 1934 Indian Reorganization Act. The BIA sent a tribal affairs specialist to help them create a constitution and bylaws as well as a corporate business charter. Of the one thousand Indians in Florida, approximately six hundred lived on three federal reservations and were most amenable to establishing a tribal government. Balloting was overwhelmingly in favor of the proposed documents, and the Seminole Tribe of Florida was officially recognized by the secretary of the interior on 12 August 1957.[34] Most Miccosukees living along the Tamiami Trail declined to join the new tribe. Initially, the ultraconservative elders wanted nothing to do with the federal government, but younger men saw a lingering threat of termination; they soon rallied behind Buffalo Tiger to seek recognition as a separate tribe with its own land and government. At that time the old medicine man Ingraham Billie and his followers broke with Buffalo Tiger and Morton Silver over the recognition issue. Given the prevailing pro-termination sentiment, the federal government was reluctant to create a new tribe. The BIA held that the Trail Indians were part of the Seminole Tribe, which adequately represented their interests. The state of Florida recognized the Miccosukee Tribe in July 1957, and negotiations were begun to lease the tribe a tract of Everglades land. This transaction was delayed and nearly scuttled, however, when a party of Miccosukees visited Cuba and met with Fidel Castro.

The Cuban episode can be attributed in part to a national meeting of Indian activists hosted by the Miccosukees in April 1959. The delegates, who claimed to represent 180,000 Indians, signed four buckskin documents detailing their grievances against the federal government and their plans to apply for membership in the United Nations. One of the individuals the Miccosukees involved in their recognition efforts was the Tuscarora activist Wallace "Mad Bear" Anderson. The Tuscarora Tribe's resistance to the New York Power Authority's efforts to build a reservoir on their reservation had recently made national headlines. Anderson was not a Tuscarora reservation leader but rather one of the new generation of Indian activists who knew how to manipulate the media for maximum impact.[35] At his urging, a "buckskin of recognition" was sent to Cuba to acknowledge Castro's revolutionary government. As a result the Castro government issued an invitation for an Indian delegation to attend the six-month anniversary of the revolution. This event proved to be a publicity bonanza for Mad Bear, who had his picture taken embracing Castro and later wrote, "They rolled out the red carpet for us, including police escort in Cadillacs, bands and machete waving campisinos [sic]."[36]

A group of eleven Miccosukees headed by Buffalo Tiger and accompanied by Morton Silver traveled to Havana for four days in July 1959.[37] They were warmly received and engaged in a round of social activities and meetings with government officials. Buffalo Tiger met with Castro only briefly but was assured that Cuba would support the Miccosukee cause in international forums. On 25 July the Miccosukees sent a letter to "his excellency Fidel Castro Ruz, Great Cuban Leader, Patriot and Liberator," thanking him for his hospitality and lauding his regime.[38] In return the Miccosukees received an oddly misspelled letter signed by Dr. Juan Orta of the Cuban foreign ministry. In part it stated: "The free Cuban Government having liberated its people from the tyranny and oppression of a dictator who was guilty of murdering and torturing thousand of innocent Cuban men, women and children, how [sic] has the opportunity to send its greetings to you and wishes for the success of the Revolutionary Government, extended by your Gobernment [sic] on January 6, 1959—in your note addressed to Dr. Fidel Castro Ruz. It is whit [sic] pleasure that the free Cuban Government takes this opportunity, in return, to formally recognize your newly established government as the duly constituted government of the Sovereign Miccosukee Seminole Nation."[39]

On returning to Florida, the Miccosukees met a storm of criticism from the press, politicians, and other Indians. A *Miami Herald* editorial was scathing in its denunciation of the trip, finding, "The Cuban gambit was the latest in a long series of headline-hunting tactics by this ill-advised group, which must embarrass the 1,000 Seminoles in Florida."[40] The *Miami Daily News* reported, "Castro's government spent more then $3,000 to entertain 11 Miccosukees for three days in July in Havana during Cuba's independence ceremonies," and flamboyant attorney Morton Silver was quoted as saying, "The Cubans love the Indians and count them as brothers."[41] The article also noted that the Miccosukees recognized Castro's new government on 6 January 1959—several hours before similar action by the United States government. Mike Osceola, a Trail Indian who had joined the Seminole Tribe and was active in its government, disavowed the trip and emphasized, "These people don't speak for us."[42] In Tallahassee the state Indian commissioner assured everyone that the reservation Seminoles were proud of their U.S. citizenship and did not seek recognition from a foreign nation.

In late 1959 Governor LeRoy Collins and the state attorney general delayed action on a Miccosukee land lease and referred the matter to a citizens' committee. The BIA continued to refuse any type of recognition for the Trail Indians, but the Miccosukee General Council steadfastly pressed its case. Citing treaty claims from the eighteenth century, the council asked for assistance from the British, Spanish, and French embassies in Washington and again threatened to take its claim to the United Nations. A group of Miccosukees appeared on NBC's Dave Garroway Show to plead their case for recognition. Commissioner Emmons, a guest on the same show, emphasized Florida's responsibility in the affair—which made Gov. Collins even more reluctant to deal with the Miccosukees. In 1960 the state cabinet voted to issue the Miccosukees a limited-use lease on a 143,620-acre tract.[43]

Despite temporarily delaying the land acquisition, Cuban recognition had the desired effect of ending federal resistance to creating a separate Miccosukee tribe. Years later Buffalo Tiger, reflecting on the quid pro quo of the situation, summarized it this way: "When Castro took over Cuba, he wanted us to come over as his guests. We went and were treated OK. When we got back the United States said, 'OK, don't go back. Promise you won't, and you will be Miccosukees.' We needed our own power, and we had to go to Cuba to get it."[44] Certainly Buffalo Tiger realized that the Indians were being used as a propaganda tool by the Castro regime, but the trip served its purpose for the Miccosukees as well.

The United States government, immersed in the Cold War, was embarrassed that one of its ethnic minorities was seeking assistance from a Communist dictator. Within hours of returning to Florida, Buffalo Tiger began receiving telephone calls from state and federal officials assuring him that recognition would be granted if he ceased contact with the Communist regime in Cuba. Action was delayed, however, until the Kennedy administration took office. In 1961 the BIA sent an experienced tribal affairs officer, Reginald Miller, to determine which of the now politically splintered Miccosukee groups would be allowed to organize. About this time Buffalo Tiger, at the urging of the AAIA and his friend Bob Mitchell, moved to sever his relationship with Morton Silver, whose extreme positions provoked or alienated government officials. Silver, in turn, put together a small group of dissidents who challenged Tiger's leadership and claimed to be true representatives of the Trail Indians. This group, composed primarily of older Indian men who resented the younger Buffalo

Tiger's rapid rise to prominence, published a newsletter, held meetings in Hialeah with their white supporters, and generally created a diversion that temporarily stalled the recognition drive. When Miller reported that the people led by Buffalo Tiger should be organized, the BIA dispatched its leading authority on forming tribal governments, Rex Quinn, who had worked so successfully with the Seminoles in 1957, to help the Miccosukees develop a constitution and business charter.

Buffalo Tiger recounts the intricacies of hammering out details for a tribal constitution. The document had to be tailored for a small traditional group with a high degree of cultural and religious homogeneity. The decision was made to forgo an elected tribal council in favor of having the entire polity decide issues such as admission to membership, voting age, and qualifications for holding office. In a concession to traditional values stemming from the Green Corn Dance, the original constitution stated that no business could be conducted unless three specified clans were represented at the deliberations (a total of at least four clans was required). Five elected officers were to serve as a Business Committee to oversee day-to-day operation of the tribe. By design, and in comparison with the constitutions developed by many Indian tribes, it was a minimal document. As Buffalo Tiger emphasizes in his narrative, it was just what his people needed at the time: it was bare bones on which meat could be added later as needed. Miccosukees had no experience with the white man's government so they had to take things slowly. Even the selection of an official name for the tribe was done with great care.

The Miccosukee constitution adopted in 1962 reflected tribal values and lifestyles as they had evolved by midcentury.[45] The retention of a high blood quantum requirement for tribal membership was one issue that would set the Miccosukees apart from most tribes. They felt strongly that anyone of less than one-half Indian blood should not be admitted. Buffalo Tiger explained that the Miccosukees and the Seminoles traced their ancestry to a common descendancy roll in Florida, so theoretically an individual Indian with at least one ancestor on that roll could join either tribe. Moreover, the Seminole constitution provided for the admission of individuals with one-quarter Indian blood by consent of the tribal council. Miccosukees believed that persons historically considered Seminoles, particularly those living on reservations, should be members of that tribe. Since there had been much more out-marriage among the Seminoles, there were likely to be fewer people of full or half blood in that group who would be eligible for Miccosukee membership. This stringent membership requirement, though broadly accepted in the early 1960s, created problems over time as more and more Miccosukees married outside the tribe and sought membership for their offspring and grandchildren. Some members of Buffalo Tiger's own family have found it necessary to enroll their children as members of the Seminole Tribe.

A Legacy of Leadership

Once recognized, the Miccosukee Tribe of Indians of Florida immediately faced a variety of problems, not least of which was a threat to the Everglades ecosystem. During the late 1960s, under Buffalo Tiger's leadership, the Miccosukees successfully opposed an attempt by Miami-Dade County to place a jetport in their vicinity.[46] Fortunately, Senator Henry M. Jackson of Washington, chairman of the Senate Interior and Insular Affairs Committee, also opposed the jetport, and the project died. The Miccosukees supported establishment of the Big Cypress National Preserve, which not only prevented the noise and air pollution of a jetport in their midst but also allowed the tribe to continue its traditional habitation and economic use rights within the preserve boundaries. Buffalo Tiger provided written testimony in support of PL 93-440.[47] But the land in which they lived was never totally free from the threat of outside polluters during Tiger's two decades as chairman. In the 1990s his successors in the tribal government initiated a major suit against state and federal governments demanding a cleanup of the mercury-laden Everglades water flowing through their lands.

The small tribe's most critical need was economic development. With funds borrowed from the Bureau of Indian Affairs, the tribe opened a restaurant and service station/grocery store on the Tamiami Trail.[48] Buffalo Tiger struggled to make it a success—his wife worked in the restaurant without pay—but these businesses provided limited employment and produced only a modest return. Several Great Society programs such as Neighborhood Youth Corps and a Community Action Program funded through the Office of Economic Opportunity also provided some employment opportunities. Still, the best-paying jobs on the reservation belonged to non-Indians who were employees of the BIA agency located at the town of Homestead, some forty miles from the main Miccosukee settlement. There had been friction with agents after Reginald Miller, who had worked with the tribe from its founding, left in 1966 for another assignment.[49]

In 1970 President Richard Nixon articulated the federal government's new commitment to a policy of Indian self-determination. This position represented the conclusion of the government's termination policy and promised a new era for the tribes. Most Indian tribes did not know exactly what this shift in policy meant, however, or how to respond. There was some limited contracting on western reservations, but no tribe was free of BIA supervision. Ironically, it would be the small and relatively obscure Miccosukee Tribe that took the lead nationally in asserting a tribe's right to run its own affairs. By 1970 Buffalo Tiger had determined that his tribe should control the operation of its school program and all other social services provided by the BIA. With the guidance of Bobo Dean, an experienced Washington-based attorney whose firm frequently represented the AAIA, the tribe proposed entering into a contract for services with the Bureau of Indian Affairs.[50] This meant that federal funds would flow directly to the Miccosukee tribal government, which could then control all expenditures. Furthermore, the Miccosukees wanted the agency in Homestead closed and its functions and equipment transferred to the tribal government.

A letter from Acting Commissioner Anthony P. Lincoln in January 1971 was the key document committing the BIA to Miccosukee control of the school.[51] This move exacerbated a major policy debate within the BIA, pitting old-timers who resisted granting Indians control over their own affairs against more progressive administrators. At one point attorney Dean wrote to Buffalo Tiger: "I am now convinced there is internecine strife" in the agency; this surmise was confirmed when Commissioner of Indian Affairs Louis R. Bruce informed Dean that the Department of Interior had issued instructions not to contract.[52] Dean recalled that there were numerous legal as well as political obstacles. The associate solicitor for Indian affairs raised questions about the legality of contracting that had to be rebutted. There was also resistance in Congress to dispensing funds directly to tribes, but that was defeated with the support of Senator Lawton Chiles of Florida.[53] At a more personal level, patronizing BIA bureaucrats constantly called the Miccosukee chairman "Buffalo" or "Buff," and that struck the tribe's attorney as being inappropriate. Therefore he always made it a point to address the chairman as "Mr. Tiger" in their presence.[54]

With the support of Commissioner Bruce, himself an Indian, a Miccosukee contract was approved for some twenty-three thousand dollars to cover a few months' expenditures at the school. Thus the Miccosukees became the first American Indian tribe to begin direct comprehensive contracting with the federal government. On 12 June 1971 Commissioner Bruce met with Buffalo Tiger to sign the contract, ushering in a new era for Indian tribes.[55] It was a modest beginning for what was to become an enormous conduit for funds from Washington. For example, the contract for fiscal year 1972 jumped to $300,000 and covered virtually every aspect of social services for the Miccosukee Tribe. By fiscal year 1993 the amount had risen to $700,000 and included a Title I bilingual education program. The Miccosukees' success in administering these funds was cited when Congress enacted the 1975 Indian Self-Determination Act (PL 93-638), which allowed other tribes to emulate the Miccosukee example. The Miccosukees formed a tribal business corporation to handle the influx of federal monies. This reversal of fortune placed Buffalo Tiger, as chairman of the Business Council, in charge of a large annual budget with substantial administrative overhead costs; consequently, his personal financial situation improved dramatically.

In 1968 the Miccosukee chairman met with the elected leaders of three other federally recognized tribes—the Mississippi Choctaws, Seminoles, and Eastern Band of Cherokees—to organize the United Southeastern Tribes (USET) as a regional advocacy organization for federally recognized tribes east of the Mississippi River.[56] Buffalo Tiger served as an officer or board member of USET for more than seventeen years. In its first decade the organization grew rapidly, and its name was changed in 1979 to United South and Eastern Tribes, reflecting the addition of many tribes from the Northeast. USET leaders realized that their tribes were small in population and lacked the political strength to influence the quality of services provided by the federal government. As a unified group, though, they could lobby more effectively in Washington, and their first successful effort was to improve health services for the tribes. Because IHS programs were found primarily among western "Indian Country" tribes, USET claimed that tribes in the southeastern United States were inadequately served. In 1971 an IHS Program Office was established to serve USET members; since 1975 the offices of both organizations have been located in Nashville. Today USET represents some thirty tribes from Texas to the Canadian border.

By a 1974 executive order Governor Reubin O'd Askew established the Florida Governor's Council on Indian Affairs to advise his office on issues of concern to Indian people in the state. Three years earlier Buffalo Tiger had suggested the establishment of a State Indian Commission in a letter to Governor Askew.[57] The council was co-chaired by the leaders of the two federally recognized tribes, and its fifteen members were both Indian and non-Indian gubernatorial appointees. With a permanent staff and small budget the FGCIA mounted an effective lobbying effort with both the executive and legislative branches of state government and provided an Indian perspective on issues ranging from university scholarships for Indian youths and minority contracting to control of development affecting environmentally sensitive lands and prehistoric burial sites. The council also acted as a conduit for federal employment programs and training grants for Indian citizens who are not members of Florida's federally recognized tribes, a function that occasionally led to friction between the Seminole and Miccosukee members and nonrecognized Indian groups in the state. On balance, though, the Governor's Council was recognized as a significant effort to provide all Indian citizens in Florida a greater voice in state government. As co-chairman from 1974 to 1985, Buffalo Tiger became a familiar figure in the state capital.

Buffalo Tiger had already begun to make a name for himself on the national scene. In 1967 he appeared before the Senate Special Subcommittee on Indian Education, chaired by Senator Robert F. Kennedy of New York. The committee was seeking examples of successful Indian-run educational programs and was interested in hearing about the Miccosukee school. In response to Kennedy's questions, Tiger detailed the tribe's effort to maintain cultural values while preparing youngsters to survive in the outside world:

> The Indian people realized, particularly the Miccosukee realized, that they are afraid they will lose out as Indians; in other words, they do not want to lose their religion, they do not want to lose their beliefs, their customs. We asked the United States: Could we keep this if we accept education, or be educated, to be able to get a job in town among other people? So the United States promised the Miccosukee people we are not going to take away anything away from your people. We are not going to destroy the people. . . . So the Indian people accepted this idea. So then they discussed the school programs, the Bureau of Indian Affairs said, and we said: "Could we teach the Indian children in the

classroom our Indian beliefs, like our religion and history as Indians?" They said, "Yes, you can have Indian teachers, however you want it. You can go into the classroom and teach them an hour or two hours a day. Meantime, we will be teaching the English, learn how to write or speak, learn how to speak English." So we did. When we started school, we have two Indian people who speak our language, taught English with these youngsters. We started in the sixth grade at the beginning. We only have about twenty, twenty-two, to start off. And an interpreter has to be used so teachers can understand the youngsters. We had a problem to get going, because we are so far behind in education. So the first year, we wasted time trying to teach youngsters to sit on the chair, to sit at the counter, to use your forks, go to the bathroom, teach them to use the bathroom, wash their hands, all that. It takes the first year. After that, they begin to learn how to read and write.[58]

Unlike government-run Indian education programs on western reservations, many of which had failed, Tiger believed, "It is working wonderful with us. Of course, we only have the school going five years now, and a small tribe. But it is working real good and I know from the discussions that I heard today it is real good, because other tribes do not have the schools we have."[59]

After Robert Kennedy's assassination in 1968, this study on the inadequacies of Indian education in the United States continued under the leadership of Senator Edward Kennedy of Massachusetts. Its findings were published in 1969 under the title *Indian Education: A National Tragedy, a National Challenge*. An edited version of Chairman Tiger's comments appeared in a 1971 book titled *I Have Spoken: American History through the Voices of the Indians*.[60]

As a member of the National Tribal Chairman's Association, Tiger was involved in several significant issues affecting American Indian life during the 1970s. Like most leaders of federally recognized tribes, he was opposed to the radical actions of groups such as the American Indian Movement (AIM), which occupied the BIA building in Washington in 1972. In a telegram to Commissioner Bruce he offered, "As chairman of the Miccosukee Tribe of Indians of Florida and member of the National Tribal Chairman's Association (representing the Eastern United States) the intentions of the group in the Trail of Broken Treaties movement presently taking place in Washington DC have not been made known to me. And I therefore cannot support action of this group. It is my belief that there is no involvement from Florida tribes or from tribes represented by the officers of the National Tribal Chairman's Association. Realizing there are problems and needs among all Indian people, experience has proven to me that combined efforts can be made through consultation with Government. I feel it is the responsibility of the Chairmans to express the desire and needs of their people."[61] This statement confirmed that the Miccosukee Tribe would depend on negotiation rather than confrontation to achieve its ends.

The usefulness of retaining cordial relations with state officials was demonstrated when the Miccosukees and Seminoles moved to subtly undo the result of PL-280. Twenty years earlier, during the termination era, the act allowed states to assume civil and criminal jurisdiction over tribes. Unaccountably, Florida was one of the states opting to exercise legal control over its Indian inhabitants, but it had never moved aggressively in the enforcement area. In 1974 the Florida Governor's Council on Criminal Justice studied the rising crime rate on Indian reservations and recommended establishing special improvement districts so that Indian tribes could provide adequate law enforcement with the use of federal funds. Both Seminole and Miccosukee leaders often complained of problems with non-Indians entering their lands. Buffalo Tiger reported that a hit-and-run driver on the Tamiami Trail had killed his nephew, and there were instances of motorists taking gunshots at Indians from the highway. "The only serious problems we have are people coming from outside," Tiger said. "Being out in the Glades, it seems you have no law enforcement. It's open. Drug problems, crime problems get to us quicker."[62] After the Florida legislature enacted enabling statutes, both tribes became eligible for grants from the Law Enforcement Assistance Administration and other federal agencies.

In 1976 the Miccosukees established a public safety department to provide police and fire protection on the reservation; they also initiated a tribal court to exercise jurisdiction over civil offenses committed on reservation lands. Two judges preside over cases brought before this court, one assessing the case based on Miccosukee laws and customs and the other viewing it from the perspective of contemporary law. Most often sentences are meted out in accordance with traditional tribal punishment. Criminal cases are transferred to the appropriate non-Indian jurisdiction. In 2001 the Miccosukee Tribe was considering a legal challenge to recover control over criminal cases occurring on its lands.

The Miccosukee Tribe's quest for a large permanent reservation was thwarted for many years after federal recognition. Then, in 1975, Florida governor Askew, under strong pressure from sportsmen and environmental interests, asked the state attorney general for an opinion on the legality of the tribe's lease on 143,000 acres of Conservation Area 3, authorized by the state cabinet in 1960. The attorney general found that there was some doubt about the validity of the lease because of the cabinet's failure to follow proper procedures, although "the moral promise is clear."[63] The Miccosukees and Seminoles requested that the state clarify Indian rights in the license area to make them permanent and unambiguous.

Three years of negotiations failed to yield an acceptable compromise, setting the stage for a landmark suit that not only led to the acquisition of a federal reservation but also provided an economic windfall for the tribe. The Miccosukees were represented by the newly formed Washington firm Hobbs, Straus, Dean and Wilder. The litigation was brought on two grounds: damages resulting from the Water Management District's flooding of the State Indian Reservation shared by the Seminole and Miccosukee tribes, and Miccosukee claims to some five million acres of southern Florida as an executive order reservation under the so-called Macomb Treaty of 1839. The Indian Claims Commission had earlier dismissed the latter claim since the treaty was never ratified, but the specter of new litigation could cloud land titles throughout the region. After the suit was filed, the Miccosukee Tribe and the state of Florida reached a settlement. It stipulated that the tribe would receive $975,000 from the state in consideration for settling the suit and relinquishing its rights to all potential or unsettled claims based on aboriginal title and the Macomb Treaty. In addition, the Miccosukee portion of the State Indian Reservation as well as three parcels along the Tamiami Trail would be taken into trust by the secretary of the interior for the benefit of the tribe. Finally, the tribe was to receive approximately 189,000 acres of land in the Everglades under perpetual lease from the state. The state retained PL-280 civil and criminal jurisdiction in the new Miccosukee reservation lands, and all state statutes relating to alcoholic beverages, gambling, and the sale of cigarettes would be in force. Also, the state retained legal title to the leased area, which would be treated as a federal reservation for most purposes. Appearing before the Senate Select Committee on Indian Affairs, which was considering the enabling legislation, Buffalo Tiger recalled, "In 1960 the state granted us a license to most of this area. The license meant that we could stay as long as the State did not change its mind. In 1975 the State Attorney General questioned the lawfulness of the license. . . . In January 1979 we filed suit against the State because there seemed no other way to bring the negotiations to a conclusion."[64] This legislation, known as the Florida Indian Land Claims Settlement Act of 1982 (PL 97-344), passed Congress and was signed by President Ronald Reagan on 31 December 1982.[65] On the twentieth anniversary of its federal recognition the Miccosukee Tribe at long last had a federal reservation.

For many years the dramatic role played by Buffalo Tiger in establishing the Miccosukee Tribe and then thrusting it into the forefront of the Indian self-determination movement has been well known to a small group of government officials, Indian attorneys, and historians. Only now are they offering an appraisal of his work as a tribal figure as well as his stature in national Indian affairs. The individual most familiar with 25 CFR 83, the federal process for recognizing Indian tribes, which has been in place since 1978, is George Roth, the senior member in the Acknowledgment and Research Branch of the Bureau of Indian Affairs. Assessing the southeastern tribes, Roth noted: "Five tribes had federally recognized status before 1970: the Chitimacha, Mississippi Choctaw, Eastern Cherokee, Miccosukee, and Seminole. . . . The federally recognized groups all have clearly accepted tribal origins, although . . . the claimed Seminole-Miccosukee distinction projects a historical division on a more complicated modern situation."[66] The allusion here is to the "forced" recognition of the Miccosukees. Although Miccosukee recognition took place well before adoption of the federal acknowledgment regulations, the story of Buffalo Tiger's extraordinary visit to Cuba and the angst it created are near legendary within the BIA.

Washington attorney Bobo Dean has practiced American Indian law for more than three decades. He negotiated the first comprehensive contract between the BIA and an American Indian tribe and was involved in writing the Indian Self-Determination Act of 1975. He offered this view of Tiger's contributions:

> Of the contracts that took place prior to 1975, the Miccosukee tribe's contract and the various school contracts were the precedent and led the way, and that makes Buffalo's role in self-determination very important. . . . I meticulously

followed his direction. I, of course, can't speak Miccosukee. Although more Miccosukees speak English today, in the 1960s and early 1970s many older Miccosukees were not fluent in English, and Buffalo was the person who communicated their wishes. And the contracting was in fact a political issue. It was Buffalo who led the tribe and persuaded the tribe. In an election, I think in the early 1970s, there was opposition, and the vote came out for Buffalo, which was a sanction from the tribe for going forward. So I would have to say that Buffalo is far wiser and far more effective than many people that I have worked with in Indian affairs, many who are federal and some tribal officials who are far more fluent in English than he is. And I worked closely enough with him to be absolutely convinced of that.[67]

Commenting on the respect Buffalo Tiger commanded from other leaders, Dean recalled a particularly tumultuous meeting concerning the Indian Self-Determination Act in which the Miccosukee leader became a moderating influence between the chiefs and Washington bureaucrats:

It was a meeting that the Bureau had, and I believe it was after the enactment of the legislation. It was the process of developing regulations. It was one of the first meetings on that. Two tribal chairmen spoke after the Bureau explained how they were going to go about developing regulations and guidelines and so on. One of those was the chairman of the Mississippi Band of Choctaw Indians, Chief Martin, who is still their chairman. Chief Martin was an outspoken supporter of self-determination, and he basically blasted the Bureau. He put on quite a show and blasted the Bureau for trying to cut back on rights, which, of course, the Bureau has always tried to do. On the other hand, the chief of the Eastern Band of Cherokees, who was then Mr. Crowe, spoke and denounced the act and said that this is just like the termination legislation and that no consultation had taken place. He called it the Indian Self-Termination Act and did not want to have anything to do with it; the federal government should forget about this and so forth.

So you had these two significant tribal leaders taking opposite positions. It was actually a meeting, a briefing, for Eastern Area tribes. Then I remember Mr. Tiger getting up and saying, "Now, I have great respect for my good friend Chief Martin. I really think that everything that he said was very good for his tribe. And I have a lot of respect for my good friend Chief Crowe, and I think everything he said was good for his tribe. The thing that we need to be clear on is that each tribe has the right to follow its own way." His speech, which was longer than what I have reported, but that was the gist of it, calmed down that consultation meeting. The point gradually emerged that you do not have to contract if you did not want to. This was not something being forced on tribes, but it would give tribes an option to contract.

I have watched him in many instances play that kind of role, which, to me, was impressive in terms of his understanding of the people that he was dealing with, in what I could describe as wisdom, which has very little to do with formal education. I think about the old expression about educated fools. People can have many degrees but not really have perception about the people they are dealing with or not be able to communicate effectively. The tribe has gone on. It has always been in the forefront of self-determination; played a role in amendments to the act to strengthen it; submitted testimony; played roles in the development of better regulations; and continues to do that.[68]

The End of an Era

In the final years of Buffalo Tiger's chairmanship significant activities were begun to promote economic growth. First, the tribe took action against the state for damage to its lands during the construction of Interstate Highway 75 across the Everglades. Ultimately, the state settled for $2.1 million, and the tribe began operating a successful service plaza on I-75, the only such facility on a fifty-mile stretch of the cross-state highway. It also upgraded the Miccosukee Cultural Center on the Tamiami Trail, which draws thousands of domestic and foreign visitors each year to view craftsmen at work and other traditional Indian activities. Finally, the foundation was prepared for the tribe's most lucrative and controversial venture: high-stakes bingo. For years the tribe had avoided bingo and other gaming activities despite the prosperity it had brought the Seminole Tribe. Although bingo was established while Tiger was chairman, he had many misgivings about the project. The tribe entered into an agreement with British American Bingo to handle the operations. Meanwhile, however, Washington had imposed a moratorium on satellite bingo operations, that is, tribes were prohibited from operating bingo halls on nonreservation land. The issue was not resolved until Miccosukee land near Miami was accepted into federal trust status under the Indian Gaming Regulatory Act of 1988. The Miccosukee Indian Bingo Center opened in 1990, well after Tiger had left office.[69]

Thus by the mid-1980s the Miccosukee Tribe was on the cusp of major economic development. Nevertheless, at what should have been the zenith of his political popularity, Buffalo Tiger was turned out of office by the narrowest of margins. Why? First, despite the undeniable gains under his stewardship many tribal members were dissatisfied and believed their relatives the Seminoles were better off financially. Apparently, there was also resentment over the perception that Tiger's family had an unfair advantage securing tribal positions and profited unduly from tribal programs. These feelings were coupled with the traditionalists' contention that the tribe was being led too rapidly into modernization. Even the chairman's sisters, one of whom was married to a medicine man, campaigned for his removal. Disgruntled forces eventually unseated Tiger and replaced him briefly (1985–87) with Sonny Billie, a medicine man who also worked as a construction contractor. In an extremely close election with a poor turnout Buffalo Tiger received 63 votes and his opponent 66. A recount upheld the election result, and a brief period of relative political instability ensued because the Miccosukees had known only one chairman for such a long time.

In 1999 the Miccosukee Tribe opened a $50 million hotel and conference center adjacent to its gaming center west of Miami. Funds derived from gaming allow the tribe to provide improved educational facilities, health clinics, and housing for its members; the tribe can also defend its Everglades land against environmental degradation by funding litigation in federal courts. Although the annual income of Miccosukee families has increased dramatically as a result of this gaming bonanza, it has also brought a welter of community social problems associated with the sudden influx of wealth. Nevertheless, perhaps because of this new wealth, the Miccosukees have remained steadfastly opposed to taking their part of the $16 million awarded by the Indian Claims Commission in 1976. This money was to compensate descendants of Florida Indians whose land was taken after the Second Seminole War, and the amount had grown to more than $50 million before its final distribution through congressional action in 1990. In his role as a venerated tribal elder Buffalo Tiger still speaks for those Miccosukees who believe that Breathmaker's land cannot be sold and that accepting the funds would be tantamount to a sale; the issue is rarely raised in tribal meetings. It is unclear how future generations will view this matter, but for now the funds remain in a federal escrow account.[70] Today the Miccosukee Tribe is struggling to retain its old values, language, and respect for the land while integrating itself into the economy and culture of a rapidly encroaching South Florida megalopolis.

Buffalo Tiger briefly attempted a political comeback, then opted to enter business and assume the role of an elder. A generation of younger men now directs the Miccosukee tribal government. It is they and their lawyers who carry on the struggle against state and federal intrusion into the Everglades and efforts to stifle Indian gaming activities.

Today the old warrior still attends tribal council meetings, offering sage advice on matters affecting the polity and always urging the preservation of his people's cultural values. Unlike the Seminoles, who conspicuously honor the founders of their tribal government, the Miccosukees have made little effort to recognize past leaders. No statues have been cast of tribal heroes; no portraits of former chairmen adorn the council chamber; no buildings are named in their honor. Occasionally, as he passes by, mothers whisper to their children in *Eelapone*, "That is Buffalo Tiger. He is a great man who once led our people and got our land. Listen to what he says." Perhaps that is reward enough.

APPENDIX

Constructing a Life History

Harry A. Kersey Jr.

I first met Buffalo Tiger in 1978 when we served as members of the Florida Governor's Council on Indian Affairs, an advisory body to the state's chief executive on matters affecting Native peoples. Established by executive order in 1974, the council drew two-thirds of its members from the two federally recognized tribes, and it was co-chaired by the two tribal leaders. The remaining third of the members were at-large appointments, but the governor usually consulted the tribes on these appointments as well. I served as a gubernatorial appointee for ten years on the recommendation of the Seminole Tribe. As Miccosukee tribal chairman, Buffalo Tiger co-chaired the council throughout most of my tenure. During this period we developed a mutual respect based on shared interests in the advancement of Indian causes, but certainly not a close friendship. Thus it came as quite a surprise when Mr. Tiger approached me in 1988 about working with him in preparing a book. Since I was about to leave for a year in Africa as a Fulbright scholar, it was impossible for us to work together, but we agreed that Tiger should begin recording the reminiscences that were most important to him. Unfortunately, after my return several years of health problems prevented a resumption of the project, and he began working with another writer to compile a manuscript. Although I assumed that our association had ended, that was not to be the case. Tiger continued making tapes, but he and the new associate failed to achieve synergy, so the project languished until 1998. At that time the Miccosukee Tribe became involved in a complicated legal issue concerning its sovereignty and sought my services as a historical consultant. This assignment once more brought me into contact with Buffalo Tiger. Within a few months he again raised the issue of working together; I eagerly agreed, and in deference to his age and

health we embarked on an accelerated project. The first step was to identify a theoretical basis for the study.

The nature of American Indian autobiography has been the subject of
heated debate over the last half-century. Much of the confusion and division stems from a lack of understanding about the history of autobiography in the Western tradition and the role it has played in Native American
cultures. In *A History of Autobiography in Antiquity* George Misch explains
that autobiography is a relatively new development, but one that has its
roots in the need for "self assertion."[1] The very term *autobiography* is difficult to explain because it is always culturally and historically specific; the
most accurate thing one can say is that it is a "description of an individual
life by the individual himself."[2] There is a widespread misconception that
the first true autobiography was Augustine's *Confessions*, but it would be
more accurate to say that this work was the first autobiography that revealed the psychological reasoning that one attributes to one's actions.[3]
According to Misch, "In reality the channel for all the essential tendencies
of autobiography was cut in the ancient world, and Augustine's work was
not a beginning but a completion."[4] Works that deal with "self assertion"
extend beyond "written literature" and can be found in "heroic poetry."[5] By
the time the ancient civilizations of the Middle East, especially Egypt and
Babylon, started to inscribe on walls the deeds of their leaders, an acceptable form for the presentation of these life stories was well established, and
"their origin is buried in obscurity."[6] Misch finds that "nothing is told us
of the private life, except for the family tree," and that these works' only
concerns are "public activities" and accomplishments in the art of war.[7]

From Misch's findings a case can be made for similarities occurring in
precontact Indian cultures. As detailed in *Sending My Heart Back across the
Years*, Hertha Dawn Wong theorizes that traditional Native American cultures had their own form of autobiography before contact with Europeans.
She notes that "oral autobiographical narratives told to family, friends, and
community members; pictographic personal narratives painted on animal
hides, tipis, and shields; and even narrative names were all means to con-
struct and narrate a personal identity."[8]

Nevertheless, Arnold Krupat holds that "Indian autobiography is a con-
tradiction in terms."[9] That is because autobiography, in the narrowest of
definitions, requires the subject to write about his or her entire life. The
communal conception of self and the lack of any written language in the

Fig. 14. Returning from an airboat ride into the Everglades. *Left to right:* Harry Kersey, Buffalo Tiger, Ruth Kersey, Laura Kersey Lazo. Courtesy of Harry Kersey.

historic Native American cultures excluded the Indian from any auto-biographical heritage. Krupat states that these works are actually "bi-cultural composites" because of the interactive role of the Indian informant and the non-Indian editor.[10] To Krupat, Indian autobiography is the "textual equivalent of the frontier," the point at which two very different cultures come together.[11] The Indian orally relates the story of his life, and the editor "translates, . . . compiles . . . polishes, and ultimately determines the 'form' of the text in writing."[12]

William Bloodworth, in *Varieties of American Indian Autobiography*, does not dispute Krupat's assertion that in the Western model the "demands of literacy" and the cultural "concepts of self" would exclude autobiography as an indigenous form of expression.[13] Nevertheless, Bloodworth's main criterion for judging the authenticity of an Indian autobiography is whether it was reactive or proactive on the part of the Native American. The author divides Indian autobiographies into two bodies of work: ethnographic studies and "self-expressive autobiographies."[14] The majority of Indian autobiographies are what Bloodworth calls the "as-told-to" variety, in which Native Americans were asked—and often paid—to participate in a study directed by an ethnographer through questions and heavily edited.[15] To prove his point, Bloodworth cites the autobiography *Mountain Wolf Woman: Sister of Crashing Thunder*, in which anthropologist Nancy Lurie imposed on her informant's friendship to get the story of her life.[16] Even under these conditions, Bloodworth admits that there are some very good examples of "as-told-to" autobiographies, books that gave Native Americans a chance to be heard. In his opinion one of the best is *Apache Odyssey: A Journey between Two Worlds*, edited by Morris Opler.[17]

Despite all these obstacles, "authentic Native American autobiographies" were written. Bloodworth separates them into three types.[18] The first group is the "life story," written by Indians such as Charles Eastman, Standing Bear, and Long Lance, who grew up leading a traditional lifestyle, were educated in white schools, and became successful in the white world.[19] According to Bloodworth, their writings are characterized by their idyllic descriptions of Indian childhood and their gratitude for "their attainments in the white world"; such individuals "were accordingly hesitant to use their words as rhetorical coup-sticks."[20]

Bloodworth's second group consists of Native Americans such as Geronimo and Black Elk who had lived a traditional lifestyle and were then forced onto reservations. These autobiographies are characterized by the Indians' need to tell their own story. Because these nonliterate Indians needed the assistance of white collaborators in "translating, editing, and publishing," the autobiographical status can be questioned.[21] Nevertheless, Bloodworth declares that since these works were proactive steps initiated by the Native Americans themselves, they qualify as autobiographies. Bloodworth believes that the best example of an account "told through (not merely to) a sympathetic outsider" is *Black Elk Speaks*.[22] It is Black Elk's story because he and not John G. Neihardt decided what to include and how he would tell it: "Black Elk tells an intensely personal story of his inner life, of the Sioux vision quest, in a typically Indian way by refusing any credit or honor."[23]

Bloodworth's final group of Indian autobiographies is a diverse collection. They are consistent only in that the authors were born after the implementation of the federal reservation system, although only a few were born on reservations.[24] In this group are found the two most "powerful books," both of which were very successful in gaining the attention of the general public. The first is the noncollaborative autobiographical work by Kiowa author N. Scott Momaday, *The Way to Rainy Mountain* (1969). The second, a very different work, is *Lame Deer: Seeker of Visions*, published in 1972 as a collaboration by John Fire Lame Deer and Richard Erdoes.[25] *Lame Deer's* popularity derives from its ability to blend a pragmatic outlook about life and an unwavering dedication to the traditional spiritual values of the Sioux. According to Bloodworth, it contains many of the same elements as *Black Elk Speaks*; "Lame Deer's story exemplifies an unashamed drive to recover Native traditions and remain Indian."[26] Lame Deer takes on the same roles as Black Elk—spiritual leader, wise elder, and instructor—and he tells his story so that others can benefit from the wisdom he has gained: he warns of the dangers of the materialism in mainstream American society while reasserting the values of Native American traditions. Bloodworth states, "This kind of autobiography could not have been written with much chance of publication until white readers had become skeptical of their own culture."[27]

Precisely because of the nature of the "bi-cultural" or collaborative autobiographies scrutinized by Krupat and Bloodworth, the methods of white editors are worthy of examination. In *American Indian Autobiography* David H. Brumble studied the various techniques employed by editors and found a continuum of styles. On one end of the scale he has placed the "absent editor" and at the other the "self-conscious editor."[28] "Absent editors," according to Brumble, can be found in all "modern" autobiographies; their voices are silent yet they wielded a great deal of influence over their informants' responses by the kinds of questions they asked. Moreover, they influenced the final text by editing and arranging the material, thus obscuring the separation between informant and editor. Brumble does not mean that all "absent editor" autobiographies are skewed; on the contrary, many of these editors went to great lengths to preserve the Indian point of view. Included in this category are *Black Hawk*, *Two Leggings*, and *Geronimo's Story of His Life*.[29]

According to Brumble, "self-conscious" editors went beyond preserving the Native American viewpoint; they wrote explicit notes about their techniques in order to define the line between the informants and themselves.[30] These works include the collaborative effort of Yellow Wolf and

Lucullus McWhorter and that of Plenty-coups and Frank Linderman.[31] Brumble demonstrates that both McWhorter and Linderman worked in the style of a much earlier collaborator, James Willard Schultz, who wrote many "autobiographical narratives" of the Blackfeet Indians with whom he lived.[32]

In *For Those Who Come After* Krupat not only agrees with Brumble's "self-conscious" editor theory; he elaborates on the technique employed and praises the results. In Yellow Wolf and McWhorter's work, as he explains, "each chapter . . . begins with a headnote indicating the circumstances of the narration to follow, dating and placing the story of the story." In addition, there are "internal breaks in the chapters in which McWhorter describes such things as pauses of noteworthy length, hesitations, tones of voice, gestures."[33] Furthermore, McWhorter included notes, appendixes, testimonies of witnesses, and a "government report."[34] Krupat states, "McWhorter's particular collectivization of autobiography is . . . an adaptation of . . . Native American practice," in which participants verify and declare accurate the narrative of Yellow Wolf in a "mode of collective production."[35] Krupat declares that McWhorter's new technique produced a uniquely American form of collaboration. Even so, he finds that use of this method is the reason *Yellow Wolf* has been disregarded by the powers that be in history, anthropology, and American literature: "Having rejected the conception of the author as a God in his heaven, exclusively empowered to create, and the conception of the text as handed down from on high, McWhorter has paid a price."[36] Today Native American autobiography, whether created by an Indian author such as N. Scott Momaday or expressed through bicultural collaboration such as that of Yellow Wolf and McWhorter, has become a major forum for expressing the Native American worldview.

Although many of the elements examined above are present in the process that Buffalo Tiger and I have followed, our work is most consistent with the methodology of collaborative autobiography identified by anthropologist Sally Mcbeth. It is firmly grounded in the concept of life history. According to Mcbeth, "Life histories are stories that people tell about themselves. They provide a point of view on the writer's past life. They are situated in time and place. They have a teller, a listener, and an interested audience. The perspectives are fragmentary, the telling is motivated, and the resulting text is retrospective and reflective."[37] Collaboration is premised on an individual's sharing his or her life history with a trusted professional historian or anthropologist; the two of them collaborate in producing the final product. For Indian elders this process ensures that the final narrative will be both readable and reflective of the native experience. Collaborative autobiography is one response to the perceived need for greater "Native voice" in the biographical and autobiographical accounts of Indian men and women.[38] There is also recognition that, absent professional assistance and encouragement, most Indian elders would never compile their life histories. Perhaps the work most highly acclaimed for achieving this end is Julie Cruikshank's *Life Lived Like a Story: Life Stories of Three Yukon Elders.*[39]

The writing of life history is necessarily a tentative undertaking when the informant is still among us. It simply lacks the element of historical closure; it is a story unfinished. There is always the concern that something major might occur in the remaining years of an individual's life to color the interpretation of its significance—although in fact even traditional biography remains an exercise in ongoing historical revisionism: otherwise we would not have multiple examinations of Crazy Horse, Sitting Bull, Chief Joseph, Tecumseh, and other figures. If, however, we view life history as a process rather than a product, another valid rationale emerges. In telling Buffalo Tiger's story the purpose is not so much to detail the totality of a life as to transmit the fundamental cultural insights of an individual and to reveal how they tempered his actions as a person and a leader. Furthermore, the opportunity to conduct in-depth interviews with an individual, constantly refining and clarifying his ideas and judgments, is an invaluable resource, especially in this case, in which there is a paucity of personal written records. It also helps overcome any questions concerning the accuracy of the informant's memory by correlating multiple versions of the same incident gleaned from interviews over time.

Working closely with an informant can, of course, lead to another problem: the historian must guard against becoming too close to his or her subject if a degree of objectivity, or at least balance, is to be maintained in the written work. To the extent that the writer is an active collaborator in the creation of a person's life history, he or she can never be fully objective, nor is that necessarily bad. Indeed, each becomes a co-participant in the life of the other. In the process of recording and writing Buffalo Tiger's life history, a parallel account of Indian-white relations in Florida and the nation unfolded as he provided insights into a Miccosukee understanding of events and the motivations underlying them. Without such insights we are left with only those interpretations provided by government documents or other non-Indian perspectives. To take what are fundamentally Indian ways of thinking or valuing and translate them into a meaningful historical account required close communication between informant and historian.

In many ways this book defies the conventional process of creating Indian autobiography in which a historian or anthropologist systematically gathers an informant's taped accounts and then produces a historical synthesis. The tapes on which this work is based were created over a period of ten years and, until 1999–2000, were in no particular thematic or chronological sequence. In addition, many of the tapes are monologues by Buffalo Tiger; thus there were often duplications or discrepancies with the tapes of the structured interviews. That was not detrimental, however. The tapes Tiger recorded on his own reflect what he feels is important—a true Indian voice—rather than tailored responses to an academic's interrogatory. After listening to his monologues and reading the transcripts, we taped additional structured interviews designed to fill the information gaps and clarify numerous points. My research into Miccosukee history and culture, as well as a limited understanding of the language, were helpful tools in framing these questions. As noted by Vincent Crapanzano, retelling of the same information often yields additional facts or insights and allows the collaborators to negotiate the final form the narrative will take.[40]

Our most daunting task was to cobble together a coherent and historically meaningful narrative while retaining the tenor and spontaneity of the informant's own words. It was agreed that except for occasional editing for grammar, plus elimination of redundancies to make the narrative flow smoothly, the story would remain essentially in Buffalo Tiger's own syntax. In making this decision we concluded that such deviation from the literal text would in no way dilute the content. Furthermore, the repeated presentation of nonstandard English when his meaning was perfectly clear would both be patronizing and tend to perpetuate a stereotype. The spelling of Miccosukee words follows the usage taught in the tribal school. Because the tapes were recorded over a number of years, some rearranging of excerpts for clarity was also necessary. Buffalo Tiger's story is episodic, that is, it does not follow a strict chronology but rather focuses on those events and ideas he deems most important during various periods of his life. Therefore, it was decided that brief historical vignettes included in the introduction and afterword would be useful. This chronological non-Indian interpretation of Miccosukee tribal history allows readers to frame a comparison with Buffalo Tiger's highly personalized account, which appears in chapters 1 through 6.

Bridging the gulf of cultural understanding was not always easy. Nuances of language, different worldviews, and the hurdle of historical rationality impeded as we sought a common ground for interpretation. My compulsion to explain events in a cause-and-effect framework was frequently thwarted by Buffalo's account of Indian actions based primarily on emotion, feelings, and spiritual beliefs. Over time, as our informant-historian relationship matured, Buffalo Tiger taught me to conceptualize issues and understand their implications from his perspective. For the first time I began to view issues through Indian eyes, to feel as Indians felt instead of merely reporting their viewpoints. Mine was a very belated cultural epiphany, coming after many decades of intentionally detached scholarly interaction with Florida Indians, so I am honored that Buffalo Tiger selected me as his partner and historical interpreter.

Notes

Introduction

1. David H. Corkran, *The Creek Frontier, 1540–1783* (Norman: University of Oklahoma Press, 1967); John R. Swanton, *Early History of the Creek Indians and Their Neighbors*, Bureau of Ethnology, Bulletin No. 73 (Washington DC: Smithsonian Institution, 1922); Michael D. Green, *The Politics of Indian Removal: Creek Government and Society in Crisis* (Lincoln: University of Nebraska Press, 1982), 4.

2. Mary R. Haas, "Southeastern Indian Linguistics," in *Red, White, and Black: Symposium on Indians in the Old South*, ed. Charles M. Hudson (Athens: University of Georgia Press, 1971), 44–54.

3. William C. Sturtevant, "Creek into Seminole," in *North American Indians in Historical Perspective*, ed. Eleanor Burke Leacock and Nancy Oestreich Lurie (New York: Random House, 1971), 96–97.

4. Charles M. Hudson, *The Southeastern Indians* (Knoxville: University of Tennessee Press, 1976), 184–201.

5. John R. Swanton, "Social Organization and Social Usages of the Indians of the Creek Confederacy," *Bureau of American Ethnology Annual Report No. 42* (Washington DC: Government Printing Office, 1928), 171.

6. Hudson, *Southeastern Indians*, 259–69; Kathryn E. Holland Braund, "Guardians of Tradition and Handmaidens to Change: Women's Roles in Creek Economic and Social Life during the Eighteenth Century," *American Indian Quarterly* 14 (Summer 1990): 242–43.

7. Hudson, *Southeastern Indians*, 172–83.

8. Joel W. Martin, *Sacred Revolt: The Muskogees' Struggle for a New World* (Boston: Beacon Press, 1991), 24–25.

9. J. Leitch Wright Jr., *Creeks and Seminoles: The Destruction and Regeneration of the Muscogulge People* (Lincoln: University of Nebraska Press, 1986), 3.

10. Kenneth W. Porter, "The Founder of the 'Seminole Nation': Secoffee or Cowkeeper?" *Florida Historical Quarterly* 27 (April 1949): 362–84; Porter, "The Cowkeeper Dynasty of the Seminole Nation," *Florida Historical Quarterly* 30 (April 1952): 341–49.

11. Sturtevant, "Creek into Seminole," 105; Alan K. Craig and Christopher Peebles, "Ethnoecologic Change among the Seminoles, 1740–1840," *Geoscience and Man* 5 (1974): 83–96.

12. Daniel J. Littlefield Jr., *Africans and Seminoles: From Removal to Emancipation* (Westport CT: Greenwood Press, 1977); Kenneth W. Porter, "Negroes and the Seminole War," *Journal of Southern History* 30 (1964): 427–50.

13. John K. Mahon, *History of the Second Seminole War, 1835–1842* (Gainesville: University of Florida Press, 1967).

14. Clay MacCauley, *The Seminole Indians of Florida*, Bureau of American Ethnology Fifth Annual Report, 1883–1884 (Washington DC: Government Printing Office, 1887).

15. Sturtevant, "Creek into Seminole," 113–14.

16. Brent Richards Weisman, *Like Beads on a String: Culture History of the Seminole Indians in North Peninsular Florida* (Tuscaloosa: University of Alabama Press, 1989), 45.

17. MacCauley, *Seminole Indians of Florida*, 469–531.

18. Charles H. Fairbanks, *The Florida Seminole People* (Phoenix: Indian Tribal Series, 1974).

19. Alan K. Craig and David McJunkin, "Stranahan's: Last of the Seminole Trading Posts," *Florida Anthropologist* 24 (June 1971): 45–49.

20. Harry A. Kersey Jr., *Pelts, Plumes, and Hides: White Traders among the Seminole Indians, 1870–1930* (Gainesville: University Presses of Florida, 1975).

21. Harry A. Kersey Jr. and Helen M. Bannan, "Patchwork and Politics: The Evolving Roles of Florida Seminole Women in the Twentieth Century," in *Negotiators of Change: Historical Perspectives on Native American Women*, ed. Nancy Shoemaker (New York: Routledge, 1995), 193–212.

22. William Sturtevant, "A Seminole Personal Document," *Tequesta* 16 (1956): 55–75.

23. Kersey, *Pelts, Plumes, and Hides*, 114–15; Dorothy Downs, *Art of the Florida Seminoles and Miccosukee Indians* (Gainesville: University Presses of Florida, 1995).

24. Nelson Manfred Blake, *Land into Water—Water into Land: A History of Water Management in Florida* (Gainesville: University Presses of Florida, 1980), 96–107.

Afterword

1. Clark Wissler, *Indians of the United States*, rev. ed. (New York: Doubleday, 1966), 279; Robert H. Lowie, *Indians of the Plains* (Garden City NY: Natural History Press, 1963); Ake Hultkrantz, *The Religions of the American Indians*, translated by Monica Satterwell (Berkeley: University of California Press, 1979).

2. Robin Ridington, "Fox and Chickadee," in *The American Indian and the Problem of History*, ed. Calvin Martin (New York: Oxford University Press, 1987), 128–35.

3. William K. Powers, *Indians of the Northern Plains* (New York: Capricorn Books, 1973), 125–26.

4. Hudson, *Southeastern Indians*, 244–52.

5. Hudson, *Southeastern Indians*, 370.

6. Hudson, *Southeastern Indians*, 161.

7. Martin, *Sacred Revolt*, 24–25.

8. Louis Capron, *The Medicine Bundles of the Florida Seminole and the Green Corn Dance*, Bureau of American Ethnology, Bulletin No. 51 (Washington DC: Government Printing Office, 1953).

9. Capron, *Medicine Bundles*, 164, 167.

10. Capron, *Medicine Bundles*, 163, 171–72.

11. Capron, *Medicine Bundles*, 167–68.

12. William C. Sturtevant, "The Medicine Bundles and Busks of the Florida Seminole," *Florida Anthropologist* 7 (May 1954): 43–45.

13. Sturtevant, "Medicine Bundles," 32.

14. Sturtevant, "Medicine Bundles," 42.

15. William C. Sturtevant, "A Seminole Medicine Maker," in *In the Company of Man: Twenty Portraits by Anthropologists*, ed. Joseph B. Casagrande (New York: Harper, 1960), 505–32.

16. Sturtevant, "Seminole Personal Document."

17. William M. Straight, "Josie Billie: Seminole Doctor, Medicine Man, and Baptist Preacher," *Journal of the Florida Medical Association* (August 1970): 37.

18. James L. Glenn, *My Work among the Florida Seminoles*, ed. Harry A. Kersey Jr. (Gainesville: University Presses of Florida, 1982).

19. Patsy West, *The Enduring Seminoles: From Alligator Wrestling to Ecotourism* (Gainesville: University Presses of Florida, 1998).

20. Harry A. Kersey Jr., "Federal Schools and Acculturation among the Florida Seminoles, 1927–1954," *Florida Historical Quarterly* 59 (1980): 165–81.

21. Donald L. Fixico, *Termination and Relocation: Federal Indian Policy, 1945–1960* (Albuquerque: University of New Mexico Press, 1986); Larry W. Burt, *Tribalism in Crisis: Federal Indian Policy, 1953–1961* (Albuquerque: University of New Mexico Press, 1982).

22. Arthur V. Watkins, "Termination of Federal Supervision: The Removal of Re-

strictions over Indian Property and Person," *Annals of the American Academy of Political and Social Science* 311 (May 1957): 55–57.

23. U.S. Congress, *Termination of Federal Supervision over Certain Tribes of Indians: Joint Hearings before the Subcommittees of the Committee on Interior and Insular Affairs, Congress of the United States, Eighty-third Congress, Second Session, on S. 2747 and H.R. 7321, Part 8, Seminole Indians, Florida, March 1 and 2, 1954* (Washington DC: Government Printing Office, 1955), 1027.

24. U.S. Congress, *Termination*, 1087.

25. U.S. Congress, *Termination*, 1122.

26. U.S. Congress, *Termination*, 1088.

27. U.S. Congress, *Termination*, 1091.

28. U.S. Congress, *Termination*, 1093.

29. U.S. House, *Hearings before the Subcommittee on Indian Affairs of the Committee on Interior and Insular Affairs, Seminole Indians, Florida, pursuant to H. Res. 30, 6–7 April 1955*, serial no. 8, 84th Cong., 1–2.

30. U.S. House, *Hearings . . . pursuant to H. Res. 30.*

31. James Haley to Bertram Scott, 22 April 1955, quoted in Harry A. Kersey Jr., *An Assumption of Sovereignty: Social and Political Transformation among the Florida Seminoles, 1953–1979* (Lincoln: University of Nebraska Press, 1996), 48.

32. Interview with George A. Smathers, 6 November, 1992, Samuel Proctor Oral History Archives, University of Florida, Tape SEM 201A, 4.

33. Kersey, *Assumption of Sovereignty*, 26.

34. Bureau of Indian Affairs, *Constitution and Bylaws of the Seminole Tribe of Florida, Ratified August 21, 1957* (Washington DC: Government Printing Office, 1958).

35. Laurence M. Hauptman, *The Iroquois Struggle for Survival: World War II to Red Power* (Syracuse: Syracuse University Press, 1986), 163.

36. Edmund Wilson, *Apologies to the Iroquois* (New York: Octagon, 1978), 170–72.

37. Kersey, *Assumption of Sovereignty*, 182.

38. Sovereign Miccosuke Seminole Nation to Fidel Castro Rus, 25 July, 1959, Papers of Buffalo Tiger.

39. Dr. Juan Orta to Buffalo Tiger et al., 26 July 1959, Papers of Buffalo Tiger.

40. *Miami Herald*, 29 July 1959, 6A.

41. *Miami Daily News*, 4 October 1959, 8A.

42. *Miami Herald*, 4 August, 1959, 6A.

43. LaVerne Madigan, "U.S. and Florida Act on Miccosukee Lands," *Indian Affairs* 38 (October 1960): 1–2.

44. U.S. Senate, Select Committee on Indian Affairs, *Hearings on S. 2893 to Settle Certain Land Claims within the State of Florida, and for Other Purposes*, 97th Cong., 2d sess. (Washington DC: Government Printing Office, 1983), 92.

45. Bureau of Indian Affairs, *Constitution and Bylaws of the Miccosukee Tribe of Indians of Florida, Ratified December 17, 1961* (Washington DC: Government Printing Office, 1962).

46. Louis R. Bruce to Buffalo Tiger, 29 September 1969; Claude R. Kirk Jr. to S. Bobo Dean, 19 September 1969; S. Bobo Dean to Buffalo Tiger, 7 November 1969, in files of Hobbs Straus Dean and Walker (HSDW), Washington DC.

47. S. Bobo Dean to Buffalo Tiger, 30 November 1971, containing copy of Testimony of Buffalo Tiger, Chairman, Miccosukee Tribe of Indians of Florida, Before the Interior Committee, United States Senate, November 30, 1971; Nathaniel P. Reed to Buffalo Tiger; Henry M. Jackson to S. Bobo Dean, 17 September 1974; HSDW.

48. Kersey, *Assumption of Sovereignty*, 190–91.

49. Department of Interior News Release, 4 March 1966, HSDW.

50. Buffalo Tiger to Louis R. Bruce, 11 August 1970, HSDW.

51. Anthony P. Lincoln, Acting Commissioner, to Buffalo Tiger, 15 January 1971, HSDW.

52. S. Bobo Dean to Buffalo Tiger, 31 March 1971, HSDW.

53. Alan Bible to Lawton Chiles, 12 May 1971, HSDW.

54. Interview with S. Bobo Dean, 11 November 1999, Samuel Proctor Oral History Archive, University of Florida, Tape SEM 217, 7.

55. *New York Times*, 13 June 1971.

56. Information on United South and Eastern Tribes, Inc., provided in correspondence with Michael D. Tiger, Deputy Director of Nashville Area Indian Health Service, 30 June 1993.

57. Buffalo Tiger to Gov. Reubin Askew, 29 September 1971, HSDW.

58. U.S. Senate, *Hearings before the Special Subcommittee on Indian Education of the Committee on Labor and Public Welfare, United States Senate, Ninetieth Congress, First and Second Sessions, on the Study of the Education of Indian Children, Part 1, December 14 and 15, 1967, Washington D. C. and January 4, 1968, San Francisco, California* (Washington DC: Government Printing Office, 1969), 79–80.

59. U.S. Senate, *Hearings . . . on the Education of Indian Children*, 80.

60. U.S. Senate, Committee on Labor and Public Welfare, Subcommittee on Indian Education, *Indian Education: A National Tragedy, a National Challenge* (Washington DC: Government Printing Office, 1969); Virginia Irving Armstrong, comp., *I Have Spok-*

en: *American Indian History through the Voices of the Indians* (Chicago: Sage Books, 1971), 155–56.

61. Buffalo Tiger to Louis E. Bruce, 16 November 1972, HSDW.

62. *Palm Beach Post-Times*, 8 December 1974, 4B.

63. Robert W. Shevin to Gov. Reubin Askew, 11 March 1975, HSDW.

64. U.S. Senate, Select Committee on Indian Affairs, *Hearings on S. 2893*, 92.

65. U.S. *Statutes at Large* 96 (1982): 2012.

66. George Roth, "Southeastern Tribes Today," in *Indians of the Southeastern United States in the Late Twentieth Century*, ed. J. Anthony Paredes (Tuscaloosa: University of Alabama Press, 1992), 195–96.

67. Interview with Dean, 12.

68. Interview with Dean, 13–14.

69. John Dorchner, "The Great Indian Bingo War," *Miami Herald Tropic*, 31 October 1992, 12–21, 27; *Broward Review*, 23 May 1988, 14.

70. U.S. *Statutes at Large* 104 (1990): 143; Kersey, *Assumption of Sovereignty*, 198.

Appendix

1. George Misch, *A History of Autobiography in Antiquity*, translated by E. W. Dickes, 3d ed. (Cambridge: Harvard University Press, 1951), 4.

2. Misch, *History of Autobiography*, 5.

3. Misch, *History of Autobiography*, 17–18.

4. Misch, *History of Autobiography*, 17.

5. Misch, *History of Autobiography*, 19.

6. Misch, *History of Autobiography*, 19.

7. Misch, *History of Autobiography*, 25.

8. Hertha D. Wong, "Pre-literate Native American Autobiography: Forms of Personal Narrative," *Melus* 14 (1987): 25.

9. Arnold Krupat, "The Indian Autobiography: Origins, Type, and Function," in *Smoothing the Ground: Essays in Native American Oral Literature*, ed. Brian Swann (Berkeley: University of California Press, 1983), 262.

10. Krupat, "Indian Autobiography," 262.

11. Krupat, "Indian Autobiography," 263.

12. Krupat, "Indian Autobiography," 262.

13. William Bloodworth, "Varieties of American Indian Autobiography," *Melus* 5, no. 3 (1978): 70.

14. Bloodworth, "American Indian Autobiography," 67.

15. Bloodworth, "American Indian Autobiography," 68.

16. Bloodworth, "American Indian Autobiography," 69. The author includes in these objectionable "as-told-to" autobiographies *Sun Chief: The Autobiography of a Hopi Indian*, edited by Leo W. Simmons (New Haven: Yale University Press, 1942), because his subject, Don Talayesva, was not only paid but coerced to participate; and *Crashing Thunder: The Autobiography of an American Indian*, edited by Paul Radin (New York: Appleton, 1926; reprint, Lincoln: University of Nebraska Press, 1983), because his informant was also paid to participate.

17. Bloodworth, "American Indian Autobiography," 69; Morris Opler, *Apache Odyssey: A Journey between Two Worlds* (New York: Holt, Rinehart and Winston, 1969).

18. Bloodworth, "American Indian Autobiography," 67, 71.

19. Bloodworth, "American Indian Autobiography," 67, 71; Charles Eastman, *Indian Boyhood* (New York: McClure, Phillips, 1902), 72; Charles Eastman, *From the Deep Woods to Civilization: Chapters in the Autobiography of an Indian* (1916; Boston: Little, Brown, 1920), 72; Luther Standing Bear, *My People the Sioux* (Boston: Houghton Mifflin, 1928; reprint, Lincoln: University of Nebraska Press, 1975), 71; Buffalo Child Long Lance, *Long Lance* (New York: Farrar and Rinehart, 1928), 71.

20. Bloodworth, "American Indian Autobiography," 74.

21. Bloodworth, "American Indian Autobiography," 74.

22. Bloodworth, "American Indian Autobiography," 74.

23. Bloodworth, "American Indian Autobiography," 75.

24. Bloodworth, "American Indian Autobiography," 76.

25. Bloodworth, "American Indian Autobiography," 76. N. Scott Momaday actually wrote two autobiographies: *The Way to Rainy Mountain* (Albuquerque: University of New Mexico Press, 1969) and *The Names: A Memoir* (New York: Harper and Row, 1976). John Fire Lame Deer and Richard Erdoes, *Lame Deer: Seeker of Visions* (New York: Simon and Schuster, 1972).

26. Bloodworth, "American Indian Autobiography," 76.

27. Bloodworth, "American Indian Autobiography," 76.

28. David H. Brumble III, *American Indian Autobiography* (Berkeley: University of California Press, 1988), 81–82.

29. Brumble, *American Indian Autobiography*, 82. J. B. Patterson, *Black Hawk: An Autobiography*, edited by Donald Jackson (Urbana: University of Illinois Press, 1955); *Two Leggings: The Making of a Crow Warrior*, edited by Peter Nabokov (New York: Crowell, 1967); *Geronimo's Story of His Life*, edited by S. M. Barnett (New York: Duffield, 1906).

30. Brumble, *American Indian Autobiography*, 82.

31. Brumble, *American Indian Autobiography*, 82. Lucullus Virgin McWhorter, *Yellow Wolf: His Own Story* (Caldwell ID: Caxton, 1940); Frank B. Linderman, *Plenty-coups, Chief of the Crows* (Lincoln: University of Nebraska Press, 1962).

32. Brumble, *American Indian Autobiography*, 83. James Willard Schultz, *My Life as an Indian* (New York: Fawcett Columbine, 1981); Schultz, *Why Gone Those Times? Blackfoot Tales*, edited by Eugene Lee Silliman (Norman: University of Oklahoma Press, 1974); Schultz (Apikuni), *Floating on the Missouri*, edited by Eugene Lee Silliman (Norman: University of Oklahoma Press, 1979).

33. Arnold Krupat, *For Those Who Come After: A Study of Native American Autobiography* (Berkeley: University of California Press, 1985), 118.

34. Krupat, *For Those Who Come After*, 120.

35. Krupat, *For Those Who Come After*, 121–22.

36. Krupat, *For Those Who Come After*, 122.

37. Esther Burnette Horne and Sally Mcbeth, *Essie's Story: The Life and Legacy of a Shoshone Teacher* (Lincoln: University of Nebraska Press, 1999).

38. Horne and Mcbeth, *Essie's Story*.

39. Julie Cruikshank, *Life Lived Like a Story: Life Stories of Three Yukon Elders* (Lincoln: University of Nebraska Press, 1990).

40. Vincent Crapanzano, "The Life History in Anthropological Field Work," *Anthropology and Humanism Quarterly* 2, nos. 2–3 (1977): 3–7.

Index

In the Indians of the Southeast series

William Bartram on the
Southeastern Indians
Edited and annotated by
Gregory A. Waselkov and
Kathryn E. Holland Braund

Deerskins and Duffels
The Creek Indian Trade with
Anglo-America, 1685–1815
By Kathryn E. Holland Braund

Searching for the Bright Path
The Mississippi Choctaws from
Prehistory to Removal
By James Taylor Carson

Demanding the Cherokee Nation
Indian Autonomy and American Culture,
1830–1900
By Andrew Denson

Cherokee Americans
The Eastern Band of Cherokees in the
Twentieth Century
By John R. Finger

Creeks and Southerners
Biculturalism on the Early
American Frontier
By Andrew K. Frank

Choctaw Genesis, 1500–1700
By Patricia Galloway

The Southeastern Ceremonial Complex
Artifacts and Analysis
The Cottonlandia Conference
Edited by Patricia Galloway
Exhibition Catalog by David H. Dye
and Camille Wharey

The Invention of the Creek Nation,
1670–1763
By Steven C. Hahn

Bad Fruits of the Civilized Tree
Alcohol and the Sovereignty of the
Cherokee Nation
By Izumi Ishii

Epidemics and Enslavement
Biological Catastrophe in the Native
Southeast, 1492–1715
By Paul Kelton

An Assumption of Sovereignty
Social and Political Transformation among
the Florida Seminoles, 1953–1979
By Harry A. Kersey Jr.

The Caddo Chiefdoms
Caddo Economics and Politics, 700–1835
By David La Vere

The Moravian Springplace Mission to the
Cherokees, Volume 1: 1805–1813
The Moravian Springplace Mission to the
Cherokees, Volume 2: 1814–1821
Edited and with an introduction by
Rowena McClinton

Keeping the Circle
American Indian Identity in Eastern North
Carolina, 1885–2004
By Christopher Arris Oakley

Choctaws in a Revolutionary Age,
1750–1830
By Greg O'Brien

Cherokee Women
Gender and Culture Change, 1700–1835
By Theda Perdue

Printed in the United States
142913LV00003B/6/A

35TH ANNUAL
MICCOSUKEE
INDIAN ARTS FESTIVAL
—2009—

MICCOSUKEE · TRIBE OF INDIANS OF FLORIDA

DECEMBER 26TH
THROUGH JANUARY 3RD

AT THE MICCOSUKEE INDIAN VILLAGE · 9:30 AM – 5:00 PM DAILY

**Fashion Shows · Airboat Rides · Dance Performances
Arts & Crafts · Alligator Demonstrations**

ADMISSION: $10 ADULTS · $7 CHILDREN 7-12 · CHILDREN 6 & UNDER ENTER FREE

Shuttle services will be available from the Miceosukee Resort & Gaming. For service details, call 305.925.2555

$1 OFF AIRBOAT RIDE
WITH FESTIVAL ADMISSION

MILE MARKER 70, U.S. HIGHWAY 41, TAMIAMI TRAIL, MIAMI, FL 33194 · 305.223.8380 · MICCOSUKEE.COM

MICCOSUKEE · TRIBE OF INDIANS OF FLORIDA

35TH ANNUAL
MICCOSUKEE
INDIAN ARTS FESTIVAL
2009

26 DE DICIEMBRE
AL 3 DE ENERO

EN EL MICCOSUKEE INDIAN VILLAGE • 9:30 AM – 5:00 PM DIARIAMENTE

Desfiles de Moda • Paseos en Botes de Aire • Bailes Típicos
Artesanía Nativo Americana • Demostraciones de Caimanes

ENTRADA: $10 ADULTOS • $7 NIÑOS 7-12 • NIÑOS MENORES DE 6 AÑOS ENTRAN GRATIS

Servicios de transporte disponibles desde el Miccosukee Resort & Gaming. Para más información en este servicio llame al 305.925.2555

$1 DE DESCUENTO
EN LOS PASEOS EN BOTES DE AIRE
CON LA ENTRADA DEL FESTIVAL

MILE MARKER 70, U.S. HIGHWAY 41, TAMIAMI TRAIL, MIAMI, FL 33194 • 305.223.8380 • MICCOSUKEE.COM